HISTOR

Frankie

A Life Cut Short

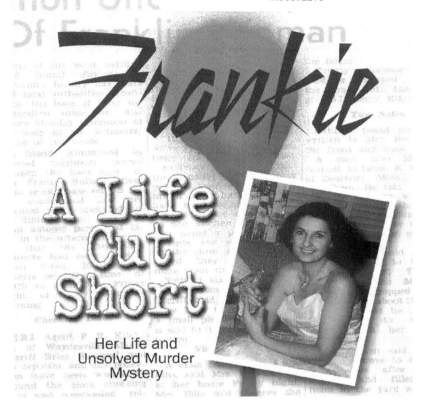

Her Life and
Unsolved Murder
Mystery

FOR DANNY,

Ronald C. Evans

2023

Ronald C. Evans

Ronald C. Evans

Cover design by Gary Vanhook

Frances S. Bullock cover photos
property of the author

Gem Capitol Publishing
PO Box 134
Franklin, NC 28744

ISBN 978-0692154441 (custom universal)

Frankie - A Life Cut Short

Table of Contents

Ronald C. Evans

Frances "Frankie" Bullock (family photos)

DEDICATION

To families of victims of unsolved homicides who have suffered the anguish of waiting for justice and closure.

To those who have suffered and survived domestic violence and abuse.

To my late cousin Charles E. Davidson whose search for justice in our relative's death inspired me to continue the quest.

Ronald C. Evans

ACKNOWLEDGEMENTS

To my wife Jean my gratitude for her tolerance and
support

My mother, Margie Stanfield Evans, for her
inspiration, personal memories, and knowledge of
family history that was invaluable for my research

Faye Lear Wells, the niece of Frances Bullock, for her
willingness to share photos, family informaton, and
support

Lt. Charles Moody, former SBI agent and special
investigator for the Macon County sheriff department,
for his assistance and sharing professional knowledge

Forensic experts Karen L. Smith and Dr. Max
Noureddine who gave freely of their time to re-
examine fifty-year-old murder evidence

Woodlawn Cemetery

Preface

Friday morning July 26, 2013 the summer weather was clear, warm, sunny, and very suitable for a task that had been fifty years overdue.

My cousin Faye Wells and I were at Woodlawn Cemetery in Franklin, North Carolina to meet with Gene Shields of the Shields Monument Company at the hillside grave of Frances S. Bullock. She was Faye's Aunt Frankie and my cousin. Shields was preparing to inscribe her date of death on the headstone beneath her date of birth that had been inscribed on the double-headstone when it was made and erected there after her husband Ebion "Ebb" Bullock died in 1960.

This day marked exactly fifty years to the day, Friday July 26, 1963, since Frances Bullock was brutally murdered during the night at her home in Franklin, a homicide that remains unsolved.

She was a Friday's Child, born on Friday and died on Friday.

Her given name was Frances, but her childhood nickname "Frankie" is how our family and many of her close friends knew her; therefore, that is how I will refer to her in writing about her, except in formal documents, or when others are quoted.

Shields had set up his large, multi-colored patio umbrella to shield him from the summer sun, along with an air compressor, tools, and templates to match the original inscriptions. He sat down on a thin, quilted blanket in front of the granite headstone, with a pack of Winston cigarettes placed nearby, and slowly set about the artful task at hand.

Meanwhile, Faye and I had retreated to the shade of a nearby large oak tree where we mused about closure, how my brother and I had been pallbearers at Frankie's funeral, what she might think of this moment, and how the unsolved story of Frankie's death had become somewhat legendary to the townsfolk and beyond. Even as we waited a local story teller was scheduled, later in the evening, to tell the horrific story of her death at the Macon County Historic Museum where her murder would be the subject of the presentation.

After a couple of hours Shields appeared finished as he came out from the shade of his umbrella, lit a cigarette, and nodded, yes, he was finished. We walked over to see the final inscription. He had perfectly duplicated the letter style of the fifty-year-old original.

The entire headstone was in good shape because Faye had cleaned the fifty-three-year-old monument a few days prior in anticipation of this event.

July 26, 2013 final inscription after 50 years
(Bulloch ancient spelling of Bullock)

Once he had finished loading his equipment, we all proceeded to the shade of another oak tree near the driveway where the vehicles were parked. He was paid for his services. He casually sat on a nearby headstone, crossed his legs, lit another cigarette, and started talking about the many stories that could be told from the graves in that cemetery as he gazed down over the rolling terrain of the sacred grounds.

He said, "I've done work at practically all the cemeteries in the county and have often thought how all those graves had stories to tell."

That gave us pause to reflect on what he said.

So, I thought to myself, "What is Frankie's story?"

Ronald C. Evans

Frankie - A Life Cut Short

Chapter 1

A 1963 Murder Mystery

It was Friday night in the small mountain town of Franklin, North Carolina, around 10 p.m. on July 26, 1963, when Frances Bullock, an attractive forty-year-old widowed brunette, arrived home in the dark of night to what would be her last night alive.

Before the sun came up the next morning she would be repeatedly stabbed in her kitchen while fighting for her life then, somehow, managed to stumble through the swinging door into the dining room before collapsing on the oak floor, near the dining table and the braided rug on which it was sitting.

Within moments, with a punctured lung and life's blood draining from her body, she took her final breath.

Her body would not be discovered until over two days later, on Monday afternoon. Her good friend Susan Wallace, who lived down the street, had become so concerned during the weekend that Monday morning, fearing that something might be wrong, summoned whoever she could think of to come and check on Frances.

Finally, shortly after lunch around 1:30 p.m., another friend of Frances Bullock, who Susan had summoned, came to check.

Flora Ellis, a registered nurse, went up the concrete back porch patio steps, across the patio to the French door. Cupping her hands around her eyes for shade from the bright sunlight, Ellis peeped in through the glass pane in the door and the window covering inside, into dining room.

There in the dining room, in the shadow of the dining table, she finally spotted the body of who she thought to be Frances Bullock sprawled on the dining room floor, most likely dead.

Could this be her friend who on Friday night, after several hours visiting, had left her house in a joyful mood, carrying a bag of onions that she had given her?

Someone called authorities. Before long, the newly elected Macon County Sheriff Brice Rowland arrived in his patrol car the siren wailing. Franklin Police Officer E.C. "Ernie" Wright also arrived.

They tried entering the house but all the doors were locked. Macon County Coroner John Kusterer had arrived, and he ordered the house sealed (by allowing no entry into the house) until the North Carolina State Bureau of Investigation arrived. They had been notified by the sheriff, who it had been decided would lead the investigation.

Once the North Carolina SBI Senior Agent P.R. Kitchen arrived, the house was un-sealed, un-locked, and they entered. Inside, they discovered a gruesome scene.

The body of Frances Bullock was found fully clothed in a bloody pink casual dress, wearing sandals, lying on her left side, and her back up against the dining table leg. There was blood around her torso on the oak floor and braided rug. She had been stabbed numerous times — she was pronounced dead at the scene.

With the investigation into her death just getting underway, the bad news of the horrible murder swept through the town and surrounding area like wildfire.

As darkness approached, and knowing a killer was on the loose, townspeople locked their doors, as fear gripped the town of Franklin. As far as anyone knew the killer could be anybody.

What in the world could have led to this event? An investigation like this was something this small town, as well as the sheriff and police departments, never had experienced. Where to start looking for suspects? A daunting task lay ahead.

Now, please, allow me to pause at this point in the story. We now know that Frances Bullock has been tragically and cruelly murdered in cold blood.

Before we continue with further details and the investigation, in order to better understand what led up to this moment let's go back — I mean way back. Let's rewind forty years and more, to where the story about Frankie really begins — back to the year 1922.

Ronald C. Evans

Chapter 2

1922 First born child

Frankie Bullock's story began on a Friday, October 6, 1922, when Frances Elizabeth Stanfield became the first-born child of Grover Cleveland and Odessa Louise Frady Stanfield in Macon County, North Carolina, in the Cullasaja community, so named for the Cullasaja River that runs through it. The river flows from the headwaters at the continental divide near Highlands to the confluence of the Little Tennessee River near Franklin.

Frankie's father, Grover, was a native of the county and that community. Her mother, Odessa, 17 years younger than her husband, was born in adjoining Jackson County, in the Greens Creek section, to Napoleon B. and Sarah Elizabeth Green Frady. Odessa and her siblings had moved to Macon County with their mother when she married a second time to William W. Estes of Cullasaja, east of Franklin.

Grover and Odessa Stanfield's first dwelling was little more than a shack on a hardscrabble farm in the Lee Cove, on a wooded mountain side in the shadow of Dills Knob overlooking the Cullasaja River. The only access to their place was by horse-drawn sled, horseback, or on foot. Water was carried from a nearby mountain spring. They depended on kerosene lamp and lantern for the nighttime and early morning chores of feeding livestock, milking, cooking, or for reading and writing at night. There was no indoor plumbing, and a footpath led to the "privy" outside.

Odessa Stanfield had a wood cook stove that had a broken oven door spring that she propped shut with a piece of the stove-wood that Grover had split from a large oak tree block into small, manageable pieces to fit in her stove. She was an excellent cook, as noted by all who had the occasion of eating at their house. They had a milk cow that provided young Frankie with nourishment when she was a child, and churned butter for Odessa's hot biscuits. There were apples from the orchard on the property that Grover tended, and her mother made apple sauce, apple butter, baked apples, tasty apple pies, and other treats for her family. In general, life was good – maybe not as good as others, but they got by.

Grover had kinfolks that lived nearby and they all shared in some of the chores – cutting firewood, tending to the orchards, and picking apples. Also, they slaughtered hogs around Thanksgiving when the weather was cold enough so the meat would not spoil before getting it dressed and seasoned for storage, or ground into sausage and canned. They usually took a share of the products for their labors.

Sometimes during apple season Grover would carry bushel baskets of the fruit down the pathway, one bushel at a time perched on his shoulder, to the river road where they could be picked up later for market or storage. His brother Harley had dug a storage tunnel all the way through the hill above his home for the apples that kept them fresh throughout the winter months.

Not many of Grover's kinfolks had a car, truck, or even had a license to drive one. His brother George Stanfield did and he bought a Ford Model-T in 1922, the same year his niece Frankie was born. On occasion George would dress in his "Sunday finest," looking dapper driving that Model T into town or to church on Sunday.

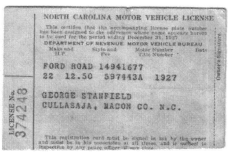

(family photos)
George Stanfield 1922 Model T Ford & his 1927 license

Moving further back in time we find that Grover Cleveland Stanfield, named for the U.S. President, was born November 11, 1888, the first-born child of Commodore and Roxie Gregory Stanfield.

At the outbreak of World War I Grover had been drafted into the U.S. Army, and traveled overseas on an over-crowded troop ship to France to fight in the war. He suffered from some health problems as a result. The Armistice Day ending the war came on Grover's 30th birthday November 11, 1918.

Upon returning home Grover engaged in farming on his father's farm and apple orchard, and did some mining in 1920. Before the war, in 1910 at age 21, he and his younger brother, Harley Stanfield, had been employed as woodcutters, boarding with other woodcutters in the Cecil Township of nearby Haywood County. Another young brother, Beulon "Buck" Stanfield, my grandfather, would soon join them.

They traveled back and forth to the log camp first by horse-drawn hack, between Franklin and Dillsboro. Wiley Hayes, an elderly, brawny, black man, who had a shoe-shine stand at City Barber Shop in Franklin, once told me as a young man he used to drive the hack across the mountain at 4 a.m. to Dillsoboro. From Dillsobro they traveled by train to Waynesville, and finally rode the company log train to the Sunburst work camp. Today Sunburst is a popular campground on Hwy 215, not too far from the Blue Ridge Parkway.

The original Stanfield properties during the early 20th century stretched along the Cullasaja River from the old Corundum Mill log dam up river, downstream to the Nickajack Bridge, near where Grover's father had a water powered grist mill. The mill most likely contained some of the abandoned Corundum Mill equipment, including the log dam, and the wooden raceway from the dam for water to turn the mill wheel. The property extended from the river inland over some bottomland, then up the mountain to their "mountain field" on the ridge of the Fishhawk Mountain range. That is where Commodore Stanfield's main apple orchard was located above the frost line and less prone to insects that could harm the developing apples. Stanfield Branch ran through the property from up on the mountain to the river.

The property had belonged to the family ever since Grover's great-grandfather, Washington Green Stanfield of Person County, North Carolina, acquired it through a land grant and had moved his family – wife Artimesia "Artie" Lipscomb Stanfield and their five children – over 300 miles in a covered wagon around 1847 to settle in this location. The log house W.G. Stanfield built is still there, although with added rooms, clapped siding, and is now in a state of dilapidation.

Silas McDowell was their neighbor, and he had developed several varieties of apples, including the "Cullasaja Apple" that was grown in the Stanfield orchard for several generations.

In 1857, Alfred B. Angel and Joseph B. Bryson deeded property for "one dollar" to P. H. P. "Pleasant" Watkins, Silas McDowell, W. G. Stanfield, James K. Gray, and H. Carpenter, as the board of trustees, to build an Episcopal Methodist Church. Following the

Civil War and Reconstruction, the Salem Episcopal Methodist Church was built in 1875. It is located down river from the Nickajack Bridge.

The Salem Cemetery is on the steep hill behind the church, where Washington Green and wife Artimesia Stanfield are buried along with many of their descendants, including Grover Stanfield. The church, now a community center, is on the National Historic Registry.

Salem Church and Cemetery (Photos R. Evans)

While Grover worked at farming, mining, and tending the apple orchard Odessa Stanfield used her skills as a good cook to keep the family fed cooking and baking farm grown products; vegetables, poultry, eggs, pork, apple pies, blackberry cobbler, and bread made from flour and cornmeal ground at Commodore Stanfield's grist mill. On occasion someone would catch a "mess" of fish from the nearby river for her to fry.

Frankie was playful there in this isolated cove and soon joined by a baby sister Nettie Mae, later on by a brother Charlie, and eventually the youngest daughter Doris Anne. The last child born was a boy, Billy, who died as an infant.

As the kids grew older they had chores to perform – tending the garden, getting in firewood, building fires in the heating and cook stoves, milking, churning butter, feeding chickens, gathering eggs, helping cook, washing dishes, cleaning house and washing clothes outside, where a large metal tub of water was heated over an open fire. Wash day was an all-day task back then.

One of the chores that Frankie and Nettie Mae shared was driving their milk cow up the slope toward Dills Knob, then over to the "mountain field" pasture on the ridge for her to graze during the day.

Late in the day they drove the cow back down to the cove to the barn for milking. The Dills Cemetery is located near Dills knob. Frankie decided to play a prank on her sister on their return to the cove. She ran ahead and hid at the cemetery then jumped out at her sister as she passed. Needless to say, that startled Nettie Mae, and later they both had a good laugh about it.

From the time I was born in November 1941 until January 1947, my family and I lived just down the path from near the entrance to the Lee Cove. That was the period just before and after World War II. When I was probably four years old, my aunt and I walked up that old path to the Lee Cove orchard. I remember going inside one of the old structures that was no longer occupied; except above me in the rafters was this very large bird with large eyes, perched there staring at me. My aunt told me it was an owl and it wouldn't harm me. The image of that owl is still vividly burned into my memory.

By the time Doris Anne was born in 1930 Grover and Odessa had moved to another house over the hill from the cove nearer to Stanfield Branch. One of the main dangers for children around these mountain homes were the poisonous copperhead snakes and rattlesnakes.

When Doris was old enough to play outside she was bitten by a snake. She and her mother were panic stricken. Grover hurriedly grabbed his little girl up in his arms and raced down the mountain, following Stanfield Branch to where it emptied into the Cullasaja River. There he crossed the suspended footbridge that spanned the river, still clutching Doris in his arms. He took Doris to the well known "rock house" on the other side. That house had been part of the Corundum Hill mining complex of the 19th century where the Leas (Lease) family lived now in the 1930s. The first telephone in the community had been located there. Doris got the necessary attention and care — and survived.

When she was old enough, Frankie started attending the two-room Salem School on a hill that overlooked the Cullasaja River and Nickajack Bridge. There were two teachers, one for the beginner's primary grade, and in the larger room a teacher for the rest of the grades. The school was within walking distance, a mile or more by the time she walked up school house hill. Rain, snow, or shine, she walked as did all the other children from Stanfield Branch, Bryson Branch, Nickajack, and Lickskillet.

When they were old enough, her brother and sisters joined Frankie and some of their cousins on the walk to and from school. They carried their lunch to school in a sack, a paper bag, some in a regular lunch bucket, or in an emptied lard bucket. Not much in those containers — sausage or ham in a leftover breakfast biscuit or two, and sometimes an apple when they were in season.

They learned the three R's (reading, writing and arithmetic) — the basics. Frankie was quick to learn and enjoyed reading, as did my mother, Margie Stanfield, who attended the same school about the same time as Frankie, although Margie was a couple of grades ahead of her. Their lifelong friendship began during that time along Stanfield Branch, where they both lived and went to school.

Charlie   Frankie   Doris   Nettie Mae

Grover and Odessa Stanfield
(family photos)

Chapter 3

Tuberculosis

During the 1930s, in the depth of the Great Depression, Frankie and her father, Grover, were both diagnosed with tuberculosis. Frankie was quarantined at the Western North Carolina Sanatorium at Black Mountain, while her father was being treated at the VA Hospital a few miles away at Oteen, near Asheville. Cold winter nights sleeping on an outdoor porch was a typical part of the treatment for her, although, it finally became necessary for the doctors to surgically remove her diseased right lung that could not be rehabilitated. She was eventually released from the facility with only one lung and recommendations of how to prepare for and live her life with that disability.

Shortly before Christmas 1941 Frankie's father sent her a package and a penny postcard from the VA Hospital in his words, but written by another's hand:

Miss Frances Stanfield　　　*Postmarked Dec 12,*
W.N.C. Sanatorium　　　*1941*
Black Mountain, N.C.
Oteen, N. Carolina

Dear Frances,
　　To-day under separate cover I am sending you a package the contents is unknown as it was sent to me from the Legion Auxiliary at Mt. Olive. Hope you will

*enjoy whatever it is. Have been looking for a letter -
from you and wondering if you are getting along fine. I
am feeling very good at this time and hope to continue.
Let me hear from you in the near future and here's
hoping this will find you feeling great.*
Love, Daddy
 E-3
Oteen, N.C.

Frankie brought the postcard to my mother in the
1960s for her to read, and then gave it to her as a
family memento.

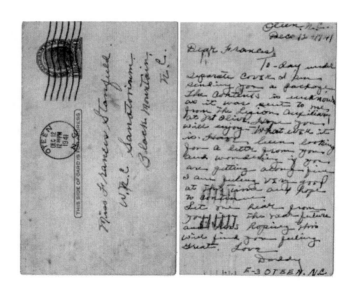

1941 penny post card from Grover

Grover Stanfield did not survive his treatment. He died at the VA hospital a few months later. He was buried with military honors at the Salem Cemetery, overlooking the Cullasaja River beside his infant son Billy, and in 1990 his wife Odessa would join them.

Military funeral and headstones Salem Cemetery

Upon Grover's death, the immense burden of supporting the family fell to his wife, Odessa. She did receive a widow's pension but it was not enough to provide for a family that had already been struggling because of the Depression and loss of support from Grover while he was hospitalized. In her first winter she had little to feed the family or wood for heat. Some gracious, kind neighbors brought her gifts of firewood to help heat their little house where they had moved near her mother's property.

Meanwhile, Frankie was released from the Black Mountain sanatorium and was living with her Granny Estes.

Frankie, who was known for a fiery temper, had some kind of squabble with her Granny Estes. As a result, Frankie was sent to live with her Grandma Stanfield and "Aunt Mae" Stanfield, and there — she found solace.

Grandma Stanfield

Aunt Mae Stanfield

Frankie - A Life Cut Short

Grover and Odessa Stanfield's teenage children

Frankie   Nettie Mae

Charlie   (family photos)   Doris

Ronald C. Evans

Chapter 4

Family Marriages

Nettie Mae Stanfield sought employment up north and luckily found a job during World War II as an aircraft construction inspector in Trenton, New Jersey, and with a telephone company.

In 1944 she married Rev. Robert A. Lear, a Methodist minister and widower with two daughters, Barbara and Betty Lear. He and Nettie Mae operated the Windy Hill Dairy Farm for many years in Burlington, New Jersey. They later had a daughter, Faye.

Frankie followed suit to travel up north, and at one point spent time in Pennsylvania with her aunt Minnie Stanfield Davidson's family. She also visited in New Jersey with her sister Nettie Mae, Robert, and their daughters.

While living in New Jersey, Frankie met William H. "Bill" Stark, who had somewhat of a questionable background according to some sources. I am told that Burlington was not far from Philadelphia and was a main route for some of the crime traffic to and from New York City. Whether Bill Stark was involved there is no record — that we know of.

Regardless of his background, on January 30, 1947 they were married at the Baptist parsonage in Clayton, Georgia, twenty miles south of Frankie's hometown of Franklin. They went back up north and made their home in Florence, New Jersey, and Frankie became a housewife.

About a year later, in a 1948 letter to her first cousin Margie Evans back in Franklin, she mentions her married life as a housewife and seemed somewhat homesick for her hometown in North Carolina.

Monday 10,'48:
Dear Margie,

I'll bet this surprises you but for a year or more I've kept saying to myself, someday I'm going to write to Margie today so today I'm getting around to it. Where are you now, what are are you doing and how are the kids? I'll bet that older son of yours [Ronnie] is quite a "quiz kid" by now isn't he? Someone wrote that Lillie [Margie's sister] had gotten married. Give her my belated wishes for lots of happiness. Is C.J. [Margie's husband] still in the army? Gee, I guess I could ask a million questions. I never get any news from home. Mother's letters never have a bit of gossip. As for me, well, I don't do anything. Just stay home, cooking, cleaning, etc. I go see Nettie Mae occasionally, but not often since Bill & Nettie Mae's husband don't get along so well. Bill and I keep planning to come down but our car is one of those pieces of junk that still runs (though it's a mystery) and we don't dare take a chance of driving down in it. As soon as we get a better one though we're coming.

How's Grandma doing? Has she been well? I suppose

Mae is the same old self isn't she?
This is all for now. Please do write and tell me all about yourself and the children and I'd be tickled pink to have a picture of them especially the little girl. By the way how old is she now?
I'll be waiting to hear from you.
Love, Frances

In the early 1950s, Frankie and Bill Stark separated and she got a divorce in North Carolina — and again in Florida to make sure. She had come back to Franklin and was living with her mother Odessa, who by then was employed as a cook at Edwards Inn in the nearby mountain resort town of Highlands. Odessa traveled to and from town by bus that made daily trips there. Odessa had managed to acquire property in the Cullasaja Community, where she built a comfortable frame house near her mother and her Estes' relatives.

Odessa's youngest daughter, Doris, had still been living in Franklin, working as a waitress at Townsend's Cafe on Main Street. She boarded nearby where her first cousin [my aunt Lillie Stanfield] boarded and also worked as a waitress. Doris and the restaurant owner's son Bill Townsend began dating and later married. They lived in Maryland for awhile, and Bill eventually got a good job with the Martin-Marietta Corp. in Colorado. Doris family's residence was in Littleton, Colorado near Denver. They had three children, all boys: Allen, Paul and Stanley.

| Doris and Bill | Odessa her grandson Allen |
| & Allen | & dog |

Odessa's son Charlie was in the Army during the Korean War. He received a medical discharge and married Jean Dayton of Franklin. They lived with her parents in Franklin for awhile and then moved to Brevard, North Carolina. Later they moved to Mt. Airy, Georgia, where they built a house.

After a few years, serious troubles had developed in the marriage and they divorced. They had one child, a son, who remained with his mother after his parent's divorce. Charlie was ordered to pay child support out of his pension from the Army, and sometimes he was tardy doing so. After his divorce, Charlie married Hazel Irene Sizemore Sanders, who was previously married and had a daughter.

Later on the couple also had another daughter.

Frankie - A Life Cut Short

Charlie Stanfield

(family photo)
New Jersey Lear dairy - Family Visit
(Frankie hand on hip)

Meanwhile, Frankie became friends with Ebb Bullock of Franklin, an upstanding member of the community. Frankie and Ebb Bullock were attracted to each other — for good reasons. She was an attractive divorcee and admirably intelligent. He was a good-looking bachelor with an established career with the local power company, and already had built a lovely brick house in a nice neighborhood of this small town.

Frances Bullock
(R. Evans photo)

Ebb Bullock
(family photo)

Chapter 5

From Orphanage to Electrician

Ebion Richard "Ebb" Bullock was born Sept. 25, 1911 in South Carolina to William Whorton and Sudie Belle Hardy Bullock. His father was a carpenter employer, born in February 14, 1864 in Green Sea, Horry County, South Carolina. He died suddenly, at age 53, on April 12, 1917 in Greenwood, South Carolina. His sudden death left the Bullock family in dire straits. There had been seven children, and four still lived at home. Ebb and his brother Bryson were placed in a nearby orphanage.

Jan., 1920 Census: *Ebion Bullock, 8 yrs. olds (he would be 9 yrs. old in Sept), and his brother Bryson 11 yrs. old as orphans and residents of the Connie Maxwell Orphanage of Greenwood County, S.C. Their widowed mother Sudie H. Bullock and children Willie Mae, 15, and John, 4-1/2, were all living with Sudie's widowed mother Mary E. White, age 68, head of household and her daughter 40 yr. old Cora Hardy. All listed as with no particular trade or profession.*

In 1928 Ebb's sister, Willie Mae "Bitsy" Bullock, married Ted A. Gribble. According to the 1930 census they were listed as living in the *Franklin, N.C. Township and Ted was an employee at the power plant.*

In 1931 Ebb came to the North Carolina mountains where his sister had moved. Ebb attended school in South Carolina and Franklin, and college in Brevard. One of his Franklin schoolmates, Johnny Crawford, remembered walking home from school with Ebb.

Jan., 1940 census: *Ebb R. Bullock was listed as 28 years old, single, a lodger in a residence in Franklin, N.C. Township, and working with a public utility company as an electrician. At this same time his sister Willie Mae and husband Ted Gribble with 7 month old daughter Janett, were listed as living in the Charleston Township of Swain County, N.C. where Ted was an electrician with Smoky Mt. Power & Light.*

Ted Gribble had a big influence on Ebb becoming an electrician.

Ebb was employed with the fledgling Nantahala Power & Light Co. that was an offspring of Alcoa of Tennessee and the TVA dam projects. Life was much better now for Ebb and his family. His brother, Johnny, enlisted in the Army where he became a career soldier retiring as a rank of master sergeant. Ebb's sister, Willie Mae, became a registered nurse at Angel Hospital.

Once leaving the orphanage, Ebb had "pulled himself up by his boot straps," and was successful in making something of himself.

During World War II Ebb continued his work with NP&L, eventually becoming a maintenance supervisor.

The TVA hydroelectric dam projects became vital for supplying electricity to Alcoa for the production of aluminum for the war effort. Meanwhile, NP&L was expanding their electric service into the rural areas of Macon and surrounding counties. Ebb and many others were involved in the construction and maintenance of the power lines being built in order to reach those areas.

Ebb became a member of the Masonic Lodge and Franklin Lions Club, and attended many of their civic and social functions. He was also a member of the Franklin Volunteer Fire Department.

In 1947 Ebb acquired some property on the Georgia Road near the Franklin town limits. Ebb proceeded to build a modern, two-bedroom hip-roof, ranch style brick house with locally produced hardwood oak flooring. The house was wired throughout for electric heat, which suggests his loyalty to his employer NP&L. Since he and his brother-in-law were both electricians, they probably did the wiring that still meets all of the current electric codes.

Ebb's mother, Sudie Bullock Pinson, came to live with him after the 1947 death of her second husband, John S. Pinson, in South Carolina. She kept house for Ebb. Many years later Dick Wallace, who had lived down the street from them when he was in elementary school, told me that Ebb's mother was quite a "task master," paying him a quarter to paste-wax the hardwood floor.

Ronald C. Evans

Chapter 6

Marriage to Ebb Bullock

Ebb had gladly shared the house with his mother, who was diabetic and required periodic insulin shots usually administered by Ebb's sister, Bitsy Gribble, a registered nurse at Angel Hospital in Franklin, or by another nurse, Ann Higdon, who lived across the street. Higdon's daughter, Beverly Higdon Moore, told me she had been shown how to administer the insulin shots when her mother or Bitsy were not available. However, she was not fond of the procedure and perhaps only did it on one occasion.

Ebb and Frankie were married in South Carolina in a civil ceremony. A marriage certificate dated *Nov 15, 1958 Walhalla, S.C. Oconee County the marriage of Ebb Richard Bullock of Franklin, N.C. and Frances Elizabeth Stark of Rt. 5 Franklin, N.C.* On the back of the certificate, in Frankie's handwriting, is the date of *Oct. 21, 1953*, indicating perhaps that was the date her divorce was final from Bill Stark, who later said he had not seen her since 1952.

According to her niece, Faye Lear Wells, a few years after the divorce Stark confronted her father, Robert Lear, at his dairy farm in New Jersey. He was disgruntled about Frances' divorce settlement. When the confrontation escalated, Lear ordered Stark to leave the farm.

That brick house on Wallace Street became Ebb and Frankie's home. Ebb's mother found a residence elsewhere at a house closer to her daughter Bitsy Gribble, further south on the Georgia Road.

The Bullock dining room furniture (and a few other pieces) was custom made by E.S. Purdom Furniture & Co., a small shop of craftsmen and designers in Wayah Valley of Macon County. Frankie enjoyed adding her tasteful touch to decorating their home.

Ebb's domain at the house was his workshop in the basement garage, where he parked their Mercury car, and where he could tinker with various projects of his own. Ebb also had a small den off the south side of the living room where he maintained his private office with technical periodicals related to his electrical work. He could have a quiet, private place to read and maintain their private financial accounts. Ebb had been investing in his company's stock and savings bonds, which he and Frankie continued to do.

Ebb was a member of the First Methodist Church in Franklin where Frankie joined him attending services. He continued as a member of the Franklin Volunteer Fire Dept., a member of the Franklin Lions Club, and a 32nd Degree Mason and past master of the Junaluska Lodge.

His Lodge membership gave Frankie the opportunity to join the Eastern Star. The two organizations had periodic social events they could attend together that were of a formal nature with the ladies wearing evening gowns and the gentlemen formally dressed.

Frankie delighted in dressing up and was admired as well as imppecably dressed with good taste. She was usually attired in the best brands of clothing. However, coming from a poor, farming background where money was always scarce she could be frugal as well, waiting for sales or haggling when the opportunity was provided. This, along with her keen eye for quality, would benefit her future antique business.

The Bullock's house on Georgia Rd
(J.P. Brady - 1963 SBI photos)

Ebb & Frankie with Odessa Stanfield at her home
(Family photos)

Frankie was happy to be back in Franklin, where she could spend time with her mother, Odessa.

It seems Frankie believed that drinking goat milk would somehow improve her health, as she certainly had been concerned about it following her earlier ordeal with tuberculosis treatments and surgery at the Black Mountain sanatorium. Therefore, Ebb got a couple of goats after building a barn out back of their house on Wallace Street. He fed, cared for, and milked the goats himself.

The twin Wallace boys from down the street found out about the goats and started showing up for many of the milking times.

Mack Wallace later described to me, "Ebb would get the goat up on a table to milk it."

It was a source of curiosity and entertainment for these eight year-old boys. Paul Townsend, Frankie's sister's young son who came from Colorado for a few extended visits, now says one of the things he remembers about the visits was those goats. Paul and the boys down the street became friends and played together when he was in town.

Eventually taking care of and milking the goats for the milk was not adding anything significant to Frankie's health, and had become an unnecessary chore for Ebb so they got rid of them and the barn. He gave a portion of the goat barn away to a fellow power company employee to make a playhouse for his daughter, and another portion to his mother-in-law for an outdoor storage shed near her house on the Highlands road, seven miles from the Bullock house.

Ebb and Frankie also had a grape arbor out back of the house. Those tasty, sweet grapes were delicious once in season and basking in the sun for one to go out and pluck a bunch from the vines. Frankie acquired a recipe for making wine, which she successfully used. She would offer it to special guests at their home.

Ebb had a dog named King. The dog was friendly to almost everyone. Many of the neighbors knew and liked King, except perhaps the young neighbor girl who took Wallace Street shortcut on her walk to and from school. She feared the dog, although the dog never threatened to harm her, only to bark as she passed by.

During their marriage the Bullock's traded the older Mercury car for a new light gray Mercury model. They were regular customers of a local Texaco service station that attended to service on the vehicle.

Ronald C. Evans

Chapter 7

Trouble in Paradise

Reportedly, Frankie's brother Charlie Stanfield had perpetual financial troubles, mostly of his own making. Although he had a pension from a medical discharge from the Army, he still could not get ahead. He did not have regular employment, and mostly picked up temporary jobs. He had worked for awhile at his sister and brother-in-law's dairy in New Jersey, as a caretaker of cottages in Cullasaja gorge, and at a furniture manufacturing plant in Franklin at some point.

Borrowing money with no means of payment on the horizon had become habitual. Ebb and Frankie became regular lenders until Ebb put his foot down when Charlie came asking one too many times.

Ebb refused Charlie's request telling him, "I've worked hard for my money — and it's time you started."

Charlie departed empty-handed and in a huff. Frankie was concerned. She was well aware of Charlie's violent temper that lay just below the surface of the amiable personality he portrayed most of the time. She even persuaded Ebb to sleep in the basement that night for fear Charlie might come back in a rage and try to do him harm. Ebb was not afraid, but finally gave in to the idea just to pacify Frankie's concerns.

Charlie had trouble with his borrowing practices in

his first marriage. His former wife said he was always borrowing and she was the one who would have to work and pay off the debts.

Ebb Bullock was in his late 40s and continued his normal routine at the Nantahala Power and Light Co., working side by side with his crew members that he was charged with supervising. When the tasks required more experience and risks he would step up and do the job his engineer supervisors requested of him. He was a "company man" with total loyalty, according to a fellow NP&L co-worker.

In 1960 he had developed back troubles that hindered his work, so at Frankie's insistence he took some sick leave to give his back time to heal. His friend, Charles Davidson, Frankie's first cousin, visited Ebb one day while he was still confined to bed. Charles brought Ebb some snacks and told a few of his entertaining stories.

In the meantime, a problem had developed in the switch yard at the company's Beechertown power plant in the Nantahala Gorge. That facility generates hydroelectric power from water piped down the mountain from Nantahala Lake.

Ebb's supervisor called him at home requesting his assistance. Ebb told him he would come back to work. Frankie was furious that he would risk further injury to his back, and pleaded with him not to go. Ebb went anyway, assuring her he would be okay and would be careful.

Frankie - A Life Cut Short

Frankie had made plans for later that same day to go visit her "Aunt Mae" Stanfield, and they were to go to nearby Corundum Hill Gem Mine to search for gem stones, hoping for sapphires, rubies, or whatever the slag from the old mine would produce. When Frankie arrived at the old Stanfield house on River Road near the Cullasaja River, Mae met her at the door with her usual jovial greeting.

Mae Belle Stanfield was a family icon, a favorite, who had never married. She inherited the old family home place. Mae was a pleasant, deeply religious woman who taught Sunday school at the nearby Assembly of God Church, within walking distance of her home. She had taught for a record number of years of perfect attendance at the church and was featured about it in a Franklin Press story.

1957 Miss Stanfield Reads Her Bible
Aunt Mae

(Franklin Press 1957 feature)
Aunt Mae Stanfield

39

Ronald C. Evans

I was in Aunt Mae's primary Sunday school class as a youngster, and after church I usually went to her house for Sunday dinner. Jell-O for dessert was a favorite.

Mae had worked at the Van Raalte Hosiery plant in East Franklin, where she had an equally admirable record of perfect attendance. She drove there in her small car that she parked at home in the nearby garage, which was a converted woodshed that had storage room above it that had been used as a corn crib (for storing corn).

Soon it was time for Frankie and Aunt Mae to get on to their adventure of the day at the gem mine. They were looking forward to the occasion of having fun together. They got in Frankie's car and headed back down River Road; across the steel Nickajack Bridge, up the hill passing by where the old Corundum Mill once was located, then onto the old concrete Highway 64 that led east toward Highlands. About a mile on up the highway they turned left and continued up the unpaved mountain road toward the old Corundum Hill mine site.

My great-grandfather, Andy Evans, was a foreman there when the mine was active in the late 1800s.

There they would have been greeted by whoever was managing the commercial gem mining operation for Jim Brinkman, a local gem cutter, who had leased the site for commercial purposes.

They went about processing the dirt and stones at

the site searching for that valuable gem everyone hoped to find but few did. The fun was in the search, and if they found something of value then that was a bonus.

During the afternoon a car suddenly approached the mine area, and when it stopped Jimmie Stanfield, Mae's nephew who was Frankie's first cousin, exited with a look of gloom on his normally smiling face. He came bearing bad news.

Ebb Bullock had been in a tragic accident at the power plant. He was still alive and had been taken to the hospital in Andrews in Cherokee County. The news overwhelmed Frankie and she started running but was quickly contained and transported off of Corundum hill back to Franklin.

In the meantime, Ebb's sister, Willie Mae Bitsy Gribble, a registered nurse, made her way to the Andrews hospital where she faced grim news when she went in to see Ebb for herself. He had been electrocuted while working on an extremely high voltage system in the switch yard at the power plant. His clothing had caught on fire causing third degree burns over much of his body. He needed extensive care that was not available at the Andrews facility.

Ebb was transferred to the Andrews airport where a private plane waited to take him to Durham, North Carolina and the Duke Medical Center Burn Unit for further treatment. His sister Bitsy accompanied him on the flight to offer what aid she could according to the doctor's instructions at the Andrews hospital.

Meanwhile, Frankie was being consoled by family and friends in Franklin. Her cousin Charles Davidson and wife Maxine, who had been close friends with her and Ebb, made arrangements to accompany her in a private plane to Durham. Once arriving, Charles volunteered to go back on the flight to get his car then return with clothing and anything else needed for the immediate stay at or near the hospital. Frankie did not want to leave Ebb's room once he had been diagnosed and treatment had begun. Maxine remained with her to console and tend to Frankie's needs.

Ebb's NP&L supervisor, Ernest Hyde, and wife Milton later traveled to Durham to offer whatever assistance they could provide, along with emotional support.

Ebb Bullock had been admitted to the Burn Center at Duke on Tuesday, October 11. Less than four days later all efforts to save his life failed. Ebb died at 3 a.m. on Saturday morning, October 15, 1960.

Frankie was filled with grief and shock, unable to make plans of what to do next. Charles Davidson, who had arrived back to Duke Hospital from Franklin with his car, now accompanied Frankie and his wife Maxine back to Franklin. When she arrived at her home the family made her as comfortable as possible.

Having gone through the four-day ordeal, she was still in a state of shock and exhaustion. The family did not want to leave her alone and rotated staying with her. They asked her cousin Margie Evans if she could spend a day with her, and she agreed. Margie [my mother] told me Frankie wanted to stay in bed, most likely sedated by doctor's orders, but finally requested a grilled cheese sandwich, which she made for her.

Frankie's clothing that she had worn while in the hospital with Ebb had an odd stench so Margie took them to the wash room area of the basement and washed them, then hung them on the outside clothes line to dry.

Ebb's sister Bitsy started notifying their other siblings and relatives of his death, while consoling their mother Sudie. Ebb had three sisters and three brothers, five of whom lived out of town. One brother lived in Pennsylvania, another in San Diego, and the youngest brother Johnny in New Orleans.

Funeral arrangements were made with services to be held at the First Methodist Church conducted by the pastor Rev. Robert Early and the Rev. Fred Sorrells, Frankie's mother's pastor. Pallbearers were employees of NP&L and Charles Davidson.

My grandfather and I attended Ebb's funeral. As the service concluded, Frankie, who was dressed in black, closely followed Ebb's casket as it was removed from the church sanctuary with her eyes fixated on it.

Graveside services at Woodlawn Cemetery were administered by the Junaluska Masonic Lodge with members of the lodge as pallbearers.

Chapter 8

Electrocution controversy

Some controversy arose as to how and why Ebb Bullock was electrocuted in an area that was supposed to have been cleared safe for him to be working. Had the extremely high voltage been turned off before he began his work and was turned back on too soon, before he finished in the danger area?

Did he purposely expose himself to the high voltage as a suicide attempt? The answer, if ever known, was never reported to the public.

There were other employees at the scene when the accident happened. Evin Hogsed, one of Ebb's crew members, later told a nephew that he saw Ebb's foot slip, causing him to fall into the high voltage that set his clothing on fire. John Bulgin, who was Ebb's good friend and fellow lodge member, quickly got a fire extinguisher to put out the clothing fire as Ebb lay on the ground after his fall.

The death certificate at Duke Hospital, signed Oct. 16, 1960 by Dr. Robert J. Flemma, MD who attended Ebion Bullock's injury, states:

He died of renal failure and third degree burns occurring when "Patient slipped while working near electrical setup which ignited clothing".

During the visitation period at Bryant Funeral Home in Franklin, Frankie, in her grief, confronted Ebb's supervisor as he came through the receiving line. He had been the one who called Ebb back to work to help on a project where he felt Ebb was needed. It had made for a tense moment for him, and for those within earshot of insinuations she had leveled.

Afterward, he asked Frankie's cousin, "Why would she blame me?"

"Well, I guess she just had to blame someone" was the reply.

He and his wife had been so horrified about the accident that they had made the trip to Duke Hospital to offer what help they could.

As she began to recover from the shock of Ebb's death, and regain her stamina, Frankie arranged for a headstone for Ebb's grave at Woodlawn Cemetery. His reserved plot was among several of the NP&L staff who had pre-purchased them, and perhaps this is what Ebb had done. At the time of his death his mother requested that his given name "Ebion" and the ancient spelling of "Bulloch" be inscribed. Bowing to her mother-in-law's wishes, Frankie added her name "Frances" and her date of birth, with a blank space for her date of death to be added someday in the distant future.

Frankie started handling the affairs concerning Ebb's death and estate. She was the beneficiary of the estate as stated in their will. His employer was holding off making an insurance death benefit settlement until the possibility of suicide was ruled out.

Frankie went to the NP&L office building on Main Street in Franklin and met with the official handling this. She became vocally angry at the suggestion that Ebb had committed suicide by electrocution, especially since she witnessed that he had been called back to work still recovering from his back injury. The conversation at NP&L escalated into behavior not normally expected from her, with a tantrum of shouting, kicking and stomping her feet, and threats of a lawsuit.

Afterward, Claude Bolton at NP&L confirmed arrangements for quarterly payments of $400 to be paid on a $10,000 benefit due her.

Reportedly, the question of it being a possible suicide being considered by the NP&L had remained in their files. The company was later merged with Duke Energy.

Ronald C. Evans

Chapter 9

Coping with Grief

Frankie felt lost without her husband who had been her companion and best friend. They had been living a life she always dreamed about. She still had the material things with financial support he had left her; however, not having him there created a big hole in her life.

To help compensate for this loss Frankie started reaching out first to relatives and friends, and gradually started making some new friends. Her mother was her best source for comfort, and she began visiting with relatives who lived in her mother's community where she had lived as a young girl. Her uncle Lloyd Estes and his wife Donna, and Granny Estes lived next door to her mother.

She would visit with her aunt Mae Stanfield at the old Stanfield house. She could call Lloyd or Donna Estes with messages to relay to her mother, who had no telephone. Her brother Charlie also did not have a telephone either, making it difficult to contact him except by going to his home or seeing him at their mother's house.

On her frequent trips to visit her mother on the Highlands Road she would often stop by her cousin Margie Evans' house, which was also on the Highlands Road near the Franklin town limits.

Her sister, Doris Townsend, invited Frankie to visit them in Colorado. So, in February 1961 Frankie, accompanied by her brother Charlie Stanfield, drove to the Knoxville airport near Alcoa, Tennessee to take a flight to Colorado. Charlie was to drive her car back to Franklin.

Apparently the drive across US-441 through the Great Smoky Mountains National Park in winter was eventful. She hints about this in a Delta Airline postcard to her cousin Margie she wrote while in flight. She had left Ebb's dog King at Margie's to keep while she was away.

Mrs. C.J. Evans   *Littleton, Colo.*
Rt. #5   *3:30 PM*
Franklin, N.C   *Feb. 11, 1961*
. *Dear All,*
Finally got going. I'm writing in flight. Little bumpy, but not scared. I had my quota coming over the Smokies. Charlie can tell you! Hope King is adjusting. Write later!
Love, Frances

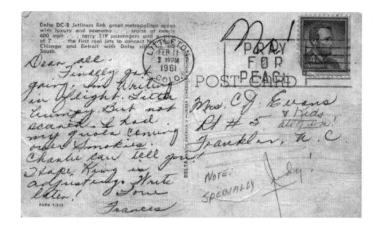

The time spent with her sister seemed to be uplifting for Frankie. When she returned to Franklin she started visiting Margie more often, usually on her way to or returning from her mother's. This became a regular pattern.

Over the next two years she made two more trips to visit Doris. On one trip to Colorado Frankie's brother Charlie, my mother, and I accompanied her to the Knoxville airport. We left before daylight and stopped in downtown Gatlinburg for breakfast. Frankie later wrote that the flight had been routed from Knoxville to Chicago then on to Denver, but she finally got there.

The last trip to visit her sister Doris' family was in the winter of 1963 when she went to Conway, Arkansas, where Doris' husband had received an assignment with the Martin-Marietta Co. U.S. Air Force Titan missile site as a Complex Supervisor.

Frankie had become a good friend with Susan Wallace, a neighbor who lived just down the street on the corner of McCoy and Wallace streets. It was convenient to stop in and visit with her. Susan's twin boys were available to mow the lawn or for other chores Frankie might need done. Frankie would open up to Susan about her personal life.

Frankie continued her friendship with her cousin Charles Davidson and his wife Maxine, with whom she and Ebb and had been good friends. She visited them quite often until she later started dating Gordon Forrester, who she knew they did not approve of because of his reputation as a heavy drinker and reported abusive nature in his former marriage. After that her visits became less frequent.

Frankie was fond of Cagle's Restaurant, where Ella Jones was one of her favorite waitresses. They shared small talk, much of it personal.

She visited with her sister-in-law Bitsy Gribble [Reed], and her mother Sudie Bullock Pinson, who was Frankie's mother-in-law, who lived nearby.

She often requested Margie's sons to mow her lawn. My brother Tommy and I rotated the chore depending on who was available. Sometimes her "Uncle Buck" Stanfield, who lived with our family, would come help her with other chores.

On one occasion, she had me come into the basement and check out Ebb's lawn mower to see if I wanted to use it. When I was finished mowing she invited me to Ebb's study telling me to look over his periodicals to see if there were some I would like to have. She knew I was interested in things related to electricity and electronics. I gladly took some and thanked her for them.

When I was still in school she had arranged, through Ebb, for me to interview for a summer job at the power company when they were hiring sons or relatives of employees for the summer months. The jobs were mostly for the brush crew clearing power line right-of-ways. I went for the interview, but apparently the vacancies were filled; regardless, I appreciated Ebb and Frankie's thoughtful gesture.

Her aunt Mae Stanfield continued to be a source of comfort for Frankie. She was always welcome at the old Stanfield house, having spent time there as a youngster. She remembered that Grandma Stanfield had been a good cook, and often cooked Sunday dinner for the preacher. Frankie told how she and one of her Stanfield cousins would slip in beforehand and sneak scrumptious samples.

Frankie befriended an older lady, Mrs. Flora Ellis, a nurse who was working in the office of Dr. Winstead of Franklin. She lived on White Oak Street near Angel Hospital. Mrs. Ellis had introduced Frankie to her daughter, Janice Helton, who was Frankie's age, and to her son, both of whom lived in Asheville. Her son was a police officer there.

In a telephone interview I had about ten years ago with Janice Helton, she recalled that when she was visiting her mother in Franklin they went to Frankie's house and saw her nice antiques, most of which were for sale.

Chapter 10

Changing the Will

Ebb Bullock's last will and testament, in addition to having bequeathed his estate to his wife, Frances Elizabeth Bullock, stipulated that if his wife's death occurred before his, or if they died at the same time or within sixty days of each other, then the estate was to be divided equally with his brother, John David Bullock, and her nephew, Paul Townsend.

Frankie legally changed the will on October 11, 1961, one year after Ebb had been admitted to Duke Hospital Burn Center, and seven months after visiting her nephew Paul Townsend's family in Colorado. She named her sister, Mrs. Robert A. Lear, as executrix and trustee of her new will and trust.

She totally removed Ebb's brother, John David Bullock, from the will. She left her nephew, Paul Townsend, as the sole heir to her estate in a trust with several stipulations, including that the full estate would not become his until age twenty-five in October 1977.

Provisions in the will gave the trustee the authority to provide funds for Paul's comfort and education, or to the trustee's discretion, any sickness, surgical operation, or any unusual emergency. Should he marry before his twenty-fifth birthday, the trustee could provide a means of obtaining a moderately priced home for him and his family.

Should Paul die before his twenty-fifth birthday then the trust would terminate with the remainder of the estate divided in equal quarters among her mother Odessa Stanfield, brother Charles Stanfield, sisters Mrs. Robert A. Lear and Mrs. William Townsend.

Chapter 11

Trading Cars

In 1962 Frankie decided to trade cars. She had been driving the second Mercury that she and Ebb had owned, so she went to Asheville to Sam's Mercury-Lincoln dealership on Patton Avenue. There she traded for a brand new 1962 tan Mercury Monterey, a luxurious car and well suited for Frankie's tastes. She looked very elegant driving it.

Some of the driveway at our home, where she often visited, was very rough, so she would park the car at a pull-off area beside the highway in front of our house. She would walk up a narrow path by my mother's flower garden, and her enormous bank of flowering "thrift" (colorful creeping phlox) that had become somewhat of a landmark and a photo-op for many tourists. Once in the front yard Frankie still had a long walk to the front porch and up the steps to the front door.

She would often appear to be a bit winded from the walk, probably due to her having only one lung. Still, she would enter the living room with her infectious smile and, once she got her breath she would launch into some event in her life. Usually it was something trivial, but other times very serious.

Sometimes her visits lasted well into the evening, and my brother Tommy would accompany her to the car with a flashlight to help guide her back down the narrow path she had followed earlier.

Alas, she soon became disgruntled with her new car. In her opinion the color was improperly matched, and demanded that the dealership do something about it. When they sort of blew her off, she started "raising Caine," pitching a temper tantrum, even getting on the floor kicking and screaming. She created such a scene the employees were afraid to approach her.

She still did not get satisfaction from the dealership, and wrote a scathing letter to the Mercury Automobile Company.

Then arrangements were made to trade her a new replacement car that met her approval.

Since she had been driving the original car for several months, when they delivered the new one, they exchanged the wheels off the new car for the old ones. For this action she sued Sam's Mercury-Lincoln in federal court and it was heard as a non-suit.

Frankie Bullock was no shrinking violet when it came to business, or whenever she thought that she had been wronged. Her outburst of anger and demands for that era were unexpected of women.

On another occasion she had an outstanding mechanics bill from M.H. McCauley she refused to pay until she was assured the problem was fixed. Mechanics were sent to Franklin to make the repair but she and the car were unavailable.

She was sued for nonpayment of the bill, so she counter-sued and it was not resolved. Whatever, the problem with the car may not have been too serious or repaired elsewhere, we don't know for sure.

While in Asheville trading cars she might have visited with Freda Holland Estes, whom she had befriended and often visited. Freda was married to Bruce Estes, one of her Granny Estes' relatives, and they had moved to Asheville. Freda and Frankie were both attractive women with similar taste in clothing, shopping, and movies. In fact, Bruce's brother Larry told me Frankie and Freda often went to movies in Asheville when she visited. Freda was one of my Franklin High School classmates.

Frankie enjoyed classic movies, and I recall seeing her with her nephew Paul at the Franklin Drive-In showing of "Gone with the Wind." She reportedly also took a niece to see that classic film.

Ronald C. Evans

Chapter 12

Buying and Selling Antiques

Frankie, along with her mother and brother, became interested in antiques. They had noticed the summer tourist shops doing well at selling mountain antiques. Well, she had the finances to invest in some if she could buy some select antiques at a low price. Her mother had been spending her winter months with her daughter, Nettie Mae Lear, at their dairy farm home in New Jersey. Nettie Mae frequently visited area flea markets there and enjoyed finding and buying items. When her mother, Odessa, returned to her home in Franklin she brought a load of them to sell at her house on the Highlands Road.

Frankie asked her young cousin, Tommy Evans, who was an art student, to make her mother an attractive "antiques" sign to post at the highway that passed in front of her mother's house. In addition to paying him for doing the sign, her mother made him a large batch of her tasty yeast rolls. She was a terrific cook and Tommy's entire family enjoyed them.

The only commercial sign painter in town, Walter "Coffee" Hall, got a little peeved at Frankie for having someone else do the sign. It seems he was very protective of his territory. She would later have Hall make her a sign.

As the summer tourist season rolled on, Frankie

and her mother were astonished at how numerous people stopped to see and purchase her mother's antiques. Frankie was beginning to find antiques at old home places around the county for her mother to sell.

Folks had them stored in attics, barns, cellars, and various places. Many were items that had been handed down from ancestors such as old spinning wheels, churns, farm utensils, plows, horse collars, etc. She got some from her aunt Mae's old Stanfield house.

Frankie had struck onto something that gave her a new lease on life. She was good at this, and passionate about dealing in antiques.

If her mother was doing that good on the Highlands Road then she might do as good or better on the Georgia Road, which was a main route into Franklin for tourists visiting the mountains or the gem mines.

She considered renting a place. Fortunately her neighbor Frank Duncan had a storage basement at his shopping center in Franklin. That would do to store excess articles, but she needed more exposure. After weighing options and advantages she decided to use her home as the shop to avoid paying rent, and other overhead expenses. It was a beginning.

The normal path to the Bullock house was to turn off Georgia Road, onto McCoy Street and immediately right on Wallace Street. She preferred customers come to the front of her house, entering on the front porch rather than her driveway and patio porch at the rear.

She contacted a grading contractor and had a

graveled driveway installed from the highway; beginning near the neighbor Faulkner's property line, then diagonally up the bank toward the front of her house, enabling traffic to pull up in front of the house where there was limited but adequate parking.

Then she opened for business. However, I don't recall seeing a sign advertising antiques in the photos of the house, but surely somewhere there was some sort of sign, perhaps made by "Coffee" Hall, to guide customers up the driveway.

She would limit her hours giving her time to search for more antiques to add to her shop, or for travel and personal time. She could also take appointments for antiques that she planned to advertise in antique periodicals.

Her brother Charlie was eager to get into the act since Frankie was requesting his help in hauling and handling some of the larger pieces that she was not physically able to move. He could also find antiques and she would buy them from him.

Between Frankie's shop and his mother's, Charlie saw that he could turn a few dollars for himself. He gradually got bigger ideas and wanted to set up a shop of his own. He lived further south on Georgia Road, so he started looking for a location, although he was too strapped for cash to do much investing.

Frankie and Charlie had a contentious relationship over the years; however, they had always somehow managed to bury the hatchet and move on as most siblings do. Perhaps establishing three antique shops somewhat spread out might benefit all three.

Frankie really did not need to get into business for the money. She was well set up from Ebb's accidental death benefits, and their longtime investments; however, she did need something that would be gratifying, and this appealed to her.

As she got more involved in finding antiques, and with her taste and keen eye for quality she started dealing in higher-end items, including family heirlooms and valuable gemstones, all of which helped fill her catalog of items she listed in out-of-town periodical publications.

Some of her prized acquisitions were a faceted Alexandrite gemstone that she thought was valued at $7,000, and a gold Elgin ladies pendant watch that she was selling for her sister-in-law, Bitsy Gribble [Reed]. The watch was a family heirloom and had been handed down through at least three generations. One of the teachers at the Salem School in Cullasaja wore a similar pendant watch when Frankie was a student there. Many of the students had admired their teacher's watch, including my mother, who had told me about it.

Frankie also had a German-made 1791 violin with case and bow she bought from her brother Charlie that she was advertising in *Hobbies - The Magazine for Collectors*.

FRANCES S. BULLOCK, Antiques

Box 471   Franklin, North Carolina

1. Beautiful Tiffany-like amethyst and gold iridescent 9" ht. ruffled top. Applied handle. Grape & flower design. $55.
2. Small 5" pitcher. Amethyst with clear foot, handle & applied band, diamond quilted, rough pontil. $75.
3. Wash bowl and pitcher, green shading to pink, perfect, Alfred Meakin, Eng. $40.
4. Old Edison phonograph with horn. Good condition except no needle. $35.
5. Sawtooth celery vase, footed. 8" high. $20.
6. Emerald green vase, rough pontil, pretty enameled flowers in red and white, gold leaves. $22.50.
7. Small hat. Cranberry cased glass in strawberry diamond pat. $15.
8. Beautiful old bronze ink well. Have to see to appreciate. $45.
9. Old album, good condition. $8.
10. Beautiful blue glass kerosene lamp. $22.50.
11. Four old copper fry pans, tin lined, long iron handles from 12" across to 6". Set $150.
12. Old Amelung case bottle, clear glass, 10". Tulip, damaged lip & stopper, so only $50. A museum piece.
13. Cut glass sugar & creamer. Nice cut. $22.
14. Priscilla pat. compote, $15.
15. Clear glass decanter with cranberry neck and flat stopper, hand on bottom in cranberry. Star pattern.
16. Plaster bust of Indian with bear necklace. Most expressive look. $42.50. Old.
17. Two old wooden butter churns. Brass bands, handles, redone, $18 each.
18. Old flow blue teapot. Leaf with acorn top. $42.
19. Brass kettle, needs cleaning. $14.
20. Old broad ax. $8.
21. Old Crewell embroidery picture 25x22". Wool on linen. Beautiful. $55.
22. Several old stereoscopes with cards. Good condition. $10 each.
23. Several old school slates, each $5.
24. Ten wooden butter molds. Assorted patterns. Lot $40.
25. 8 wooden potato mashers, nice ones. Lot $10.
26. Square wooden coffee mill, nice condition, old paper sticker still readable. $16.50.
27. Small clear glass lamp with handle. Rough pontil on bottom with words "Pat. Sept. 29, 1870." Cute. Chimney incl. $7.50.
28. Joannes Keffer violin. Made in year 1791. Guaranteed authentic. Old English Dodd bow. Good condition. Still beautiful tone. $600.
29. Lovely old quilt. Flying Geese pat. $50.

Jfyp

July, 1963 issue of Hobbies - The Magazine for Collectors

The violin would turn out to be of much more value than the gemstone.

Ronald C. Evans

Chapter 13

Moving on

As time passed and she became more involved with her antiques business, she met more people and made new friends. As one might expect, some of her new friends were single men of her age, who occasionally asked her out to dinner. Her attractive and friendly appearance drew their admiration and attention. She accepted some of the invitations and enjoyed the experience – and the attention.

One of the men she started seeing often was a bachelor Pat Cable, who was 42 at the time they began dating. He was a Post Office rural mail carrier who lived in the Cullasaja community on River Road – not far from where she grew up. He had known her for maybe fifteen years or so. They dated regularly over a two-year period. There were others, some widowers that she may have gone out with only once. Some new acquaintances became friends but she never went out with them.

She had befriended the distinguished Rev. Dr. Wilson W. Sneed, rector of St. Agnes Episcopal Church in Franklin. He had been the rector of the large St. Luke Church in Atlanta and had taken a sabbatical to further his studies at Columbia University in New York. As part of the sabbatical he had requested to be assigned to a small church in a small community before moving on to New York. He was a single man. It is unknown if Frankie's relationship with him developed beyond friendship.

There was a handsome widower who worked for the telephone company who took her out for dinner a few times.

Another older admirer was a single man who was a life insurance salesman who sold her a policy; however, once the application was processed she was turned down due to her past health record that she only had one lung. They went out for dinner once or twice.

Sometime in 1961 she met Gordon Lee Forrester, an agent-auditor with the Internal Revenue Service who worked out of the Franklin office. He was divorced. His second marriage ended after 16 years, supposedly because of his physical abusive treatment of his wife and heavy alcohol abuse.

He and his second ex-wife had one son born in 1952 before they moved to Franklin. He and his ex-wife had met when they were in college at Louisiana Tech in Ruston, Louisiana, where he received a degree in business economics in 1949. He was originally from Fredrick, Oklahoma.

Gordon Forrester had earlier marriages, actually two marriages unknown by authorities until now, as far as I know. I only uncovered this information during the course of my writing, after more than ten years of research when doing fact-checks.

In 1939 he had a brief marriage in Oklahoma when he was 18 and his bride was only 16. It appears they lied about her age and got married in another county in Oklahoma; however, that marriage was apparently annulled due her being under age. So they were married again in November 1939 with her parents granting permission. The 1940 census has the couple listed in the household of her parents, but soon their marriage ended. The county marriage records show that she married again in November 1941. Gordon Forrester soon joined the Navy. I found no record of their divorce, or if a child had been born during their brief marriage.

He was a World War II Navy veteran, enlisting in January 1942 and serving as a yeoman, and had chiefly clerical duties on the USS Hermitage, a commandeered Italian ship built in Scotland in 1925, that the United States used as a transport ship during the war. The ship was returned to Italy after the war as part of a post war agreement.

Ruston, Louisiana was his second ex-wife Marjorie's hometown, and she was from a family in the jewelry business. She was employed at the college when she returned to Ruston and later remarried. Their son, Geoffrey Forrester, lived with her in Ruston.

Gordon Forrester   (1963 Photo)
(1949 Louisiana Tech)

Forrester's third marriage in February 1962 lasted only a couple of months when they separated while living in Elizabeth City, North Carolina and divorced a year later in an Alabama "quickie" divorce Gordon filed In April 1963. His third ex-wife, Betty Sue, said he could be physically and verbally abusive when drinking.

Gordon Forrester was an avid golfer, although he had chronic back pain for which he was receiving treatment. He had played golf while living in Franklin at the Franklin Lodge and Golf Course, owned by Frank Duncan, Frankie's neighbor. He also played on return visits to see her.

In Franklin, Forrester played with several local men, two of whom I spoke with about him. Bob Moore remembered Forrester but didn't really know him that well or anything about his private life. Tommy Angel II said Forrester used to come over on Sunday and play, but he too didn't know much about him. Before his divorce from Marjorie they had rented a house from Dr. Furman Angel near where both Angel and Moore lived on Golf View Drive. This was temporary while waiting to start building a house in a new development at Forest Hills subdivision off of Womack Street where they had already bought the lot. Later the lot was sold to Joe and Nell Gibson as part of the Forrester's divorce proceedings. Joe Gibson and his wife had just returned to Franklin after his stint in the U.S. Air Force. Gibson's father had made them aware the property was available. They built a house there.

Frankie had been noticed by some of the patrons of the golf course swimming pool sitting on a nearby bench, probably waiting for Gordon to finish his round of golf. He played golf wherever he was stationed, including Elizabeth City.

In a later interview Forrester recalled that he first started dating Frances Bullock in December 1961, just a few months before his marriage to his third wife, Betty Sue, and they soon separated. Then he started dating Frances again.

Ronald C. Evans

Elizabeth City
(1963 IRS office - waterfront)

Frankie - ocean side
(R. Evans photo)

Chapter 14
Enter John Peterson

Relatives started noticing a change in Frankie's behavior during this time period when she was dating. She seemed to be hiding something from them and sometimes got caught in fabrications. Pat Cable, one of the men she had been out with over a couple years, said she was imaginative and untruthful, but that apparently had not deterred him from continuing to go out with her.

Margie Evans was her first cousin with whom Frankie had become very close after Ebb Bullock's death. Margie started noticing these changes. On one occasion Frankie was hesitant about her first date with Gordon Forrester. She told Margie he was rumored to have "beat his former wife," and was violent when drinking. She enlisted Margie's assistance, telling her that she feared the date because of his reputation, and if she had not called Margie by eleven o'clock that night would she please call the police.

Frankie did call telling Margie, "He was a perfect gentleman."

Sometime after one of her plane trips to visit her sister in Denver she told Margie she had met this wonderful man named John Peterson on the plane and she really liked him. Soon she came to Margie's to tell her more about the man and how he had been contacting her. On one occasion in November 1961

Frankie brought Margie a half-dozen red roses from a dozen that he had sent her, and she wanted to share them with her. A neighbor woman had just died, so Margie, who as an avid gardener and not really that fond of cut flowers, took the roses to the neighbor's house where they were having a wake.

Still another time Frankie's brother, Charlie Stanfield, called Margie one day asking if Frankie was at her house. No, she was not was Margie's reply. He said a man named John had arrived at Frankie's house in a taxi from Asheville and had come to see her. Margie asked Charlie what the man looked like, and he told her, he guessed he was a good-looking man.

Later that day Frankie called Margie, and told her that she was not there because she had washed her hair then went for a drive in her car with the windows down to blow-dry her hair.

At a much later date in 1963, in a conversation with Charlie and his mother, Odessa Stanfield, Margie spoke about that incident. Charlie then said that Frankie had put him up to making the call. He added there was not a man at her house the day he called.

Odessa asked her son, "Why would you do that?" He said Frankie bought him four tires for his car if he would make the call. About the dozen red roses, Charlie said that Frankie had sent them to herself.

Frankie had told someone that John Peterson was her nephew Paul Townsend's Sunday school teacher she had met on a visit with her sister in Denver.

When Paul's mother, Doris Townsend, was asked about it later, she said, "I don't know anyone by that name."

The only man she knew was a man named Gordon Forrester who came and picked up Frankie in Conway, Arkansas so they could travel back to North Carolina together in his car. Forrester had been visiting relatives in the area. It was not clear who he had been visiting, although Gordon Forrester had a brother who lived in Siloam, Arkansas, a son living in Ruston, Louisiana with his mother, and his parents lived in Fredrick, Oklahoma, in the southwest section of that state, all within reasonable driving distance of Conway, Arkansas.

According to Doris Townsend, Frankie left her home in Arkansas by car with Gordon Forrester. To further add to her deceptions, she sent Doris the receipts for two separate rooms at a motel where they stayed overnight — as if to indicate they did not share the same room. Trust was eroding away in her relationships with her sister and other family members.

Frankie's cousin, Charles Davidson, asked Margie about this man Frankie called "John." Frankie had told him that he was a general in the Army, and that she had met him in New Orleans. She later contradicted that, telling someone else that she had met him in Chicago, and to another person that she had met "John" in Philadelphia.

On one occasion when Charles and his wife Maxine returned home they found a note from Frankie written with lipstick.

It read; "John and I stopped by for a visit and sorry we missed you. We didn't have a pen."

From that point on both Margie and Charles were leery of anything she told them, and kept in touch to compare stories told them by Frankie. She was deceiving the two people who had gone out of their way to help her during the tragedy when Ebb died, and they were both disappointed in her behavior, and becoming disgusted with whatever game she was playing.

They were not the only ones being kept in the dark about Frankie's actions. Her mother did not have a telephone, and Frankie made regular visits with her. If she could not visit for awhile she would call her uncle Lloyd Estes, who lived nearby, to have him deliver a message. One particular call aroused his suspicions.

She requested he tell her mother, "I will be out of town for awhile and I will contact her when I get back."

He asked, "Where are you now?" "At home", she replied.

Estes could hear very loud music in the background and he made an accusation that she was not at home, but she insisted she was. He let it go and delivered her message.

Frankie had once made a long-distance phone call to her cousin Margie telling her she was on her way to Honolulu and would she have her son or her uncle Buck Stanfield mow her lawn. Another time she called collect from the Winston-Salem, North Carolina airport, asking if she would have her uncle Buck, who lived at Margie's house, go and check if she had left her iron on. She added that she was on her way to New York, her plane was about to leave and that she didn't have correct change the reason for the collect call.

Pat Cable, who dated her over a period of two years, said she was a light drinker, but he had never seen her intoxicated. She did make some homemade wine with grapes from the arbor outside the house, and offered it to guests on special occasions.

Was the mystery man, John Peterson, a figment of her "high" imagination, or was it an alias she had given her new suitor, Gordon Lee Forrester?

Looking back and checking facts the Peterson mystery began about the same time that Forrester came into her life in late 1961.

Forrester did not receive his divorce until April 1963, and the two had a very close relation long before that in 1961. She accompanied him to Pell City, Alabama to file for his quickie divorce. He was insisting that she marry him, and they more-or-less set the date for a wedding a few months later in June 1963.

On June 22, 1963, shortly before the wedding day, Frankie came to Margie's house to show her the heirloom engagement ring Forrester had presented to her. It was supposedly Forrester's grandmother's ring. Margie noted the small size of the diamond, and since Frankie had diminished her trust, she made a snide remark that it looked like something she had seen at the 5&10 cent store. That remark no doubt was disappointing to Frankie. Although she had been deceiving Margie, she had always maintained high respect for her ever since their childhood. Frankie soon mentioned what Margie had said about the ring to their cousin Charles Davidson, who simply reported that back to Margie. Frankie, apparently with hurt feelings, stopped her regular visits to Margie's after that.

I missed her visits that were usually entertaining while listening to her stories real or imagined. She enjoyed getting into conversations with me and my siblings and was seemingly always interested in what we were doing at the time. After that I saw her drive by our house, and she seemed to purposely not look my way; otherwise, she would have honked the car horn or waved a greeting.

Margie had seen her briefly from a distance on the Highlands Road sitting close to a man who was driving her car. When Frankie saw Margie she reached over and honked the car horn and waved, Margie said.

Sometime after Frankie's last visit to Margie's, her sister Doris called Margie from Arkansas, trying to get up with Frankie. She had been calling her house numerous times and got no answer. Margie told her she had not talked with her since she came to tell her she was getting married and had shown her the engagement ring.

Upon hearing this Doris exploded on the phone,

exclaiming, "She has told me nothing about this."

Doris had a fiery temper as well – that seemed to be a family trait for Frankie and her siblings. Doris said she was going to keep trying to reach Frankie. If Margie heard from Frankie to have her call. Later, Frankie did call Margie and told her that Doris had calmed down, and she had put her mind at ease about all that.

Doris later says that she had thought that Frankie's "high imagination" came from her time hospitalized at the Black Mountain tubuerculosis sanatorium, in isolation, with nothing else to do but read numerous books of fiction. Frankie was an avid reader.

One of Frankie's longtime friends, who had helped her and the family when she had tuburculosis, was told of the upcoming wedding. Frankie had verbally invited her to attend, so the lady bought a dress to wear especially to the event. When the wedding day came and went, and no wedding or explanation, she was not pleased.

Once Gordon Forrester applied for his quickie divorce from his third wife, and it was quickly granted, he became more insistent about his marriage to Frankie.

Forrester wanted her to marry him and come live in Elizabeth City, which is located in the far eastern area of North Carolina near sea level. On the advice of her doctor, she told Gordon she could not do that because it would be unhealthy for her because of having only one lung.

With that Forrester applied for a transfer back to the mountains. He had been reassigned to that distant post of the IRS due to some internal affairs that almost got him fired when he was in the Franklin office. He was reportedly given a chance to build some more time toward retirement but was not to have any direct contact with the public concerning their IRS issues; instead, they would find him other duties where he could contribute to their mission. His violent temper had been the root of his earlier problems, magnified by his drinking after hours.

Forrester continued pressuring Frankie about their marriage. Still, the June marriage did not take place. It appeared she was not fully committed to marrying him.

Sometime in June 1963 Frankie had another dinner date with Pat Cable. She confided in him how Forrester was insisting she marry him. Cable later made light of that, attributing it to her imaginative behavior.

Frankie   (Blue Ridge Parkway)   Gordon

Chapter 15

Events of July 1963

Frankie Bullock and Gordon Forrester were seeing each other every weekend in July. Forrester somehow managed to get to and from Franklin, or close by, from Elizabeth City for three consecutive weekends in order to be with Frankie.

Monday, July 1
• U.S. Postal ZIP codes introduced.
• The Beatles release "Twist and Shout."
Gordon Forrester was intending to visit Frankie during the Fourth of July week during his holiday time off.

Thurday, July 4
Frankie had earlier called her sister, Nettie Mae Lear, in Burlington, New Jersey, and discussed coming there for a visit. Nettie Mae informed Frankie that her young step-daughter, Betty Fejakowsky, her husband Stan, and their little girl were coming south to Franklin for their first visit to the mountains. Betty's husband Stan worked at a plant in Burlington that shut down for a week around the Fourth of July. So, Frankie decided she would stay in Franklin.

When the young family from New Jersey arrived they stayed with Odessa Stanfield, Nettie Mae's mother.

Frankie invited them to go with her and a friend on a picnic to Wayah Bald, a popular mountaintop attraction, where they could get a panoramic view of the area mountains. The next day Frankie picked them up at Odessa's house then stopped by Frankie's house where they met Gordon Forrester. He drove Frankie's four-door Mercury with her seated close to him, and Betty and her family in the back seat.

Betty's impression of Forrester, she told me, was that he was argumentative and boastful. He had commented about working in Elizabeth City and how he could make the long trip quicker across state to Franklin by taking back roads. He also bragged that in his line of work he knew things on people which enabled him to get by doing things that others would not. During the picnic Forrester made a few belligerent comments, and Betty got the impression the remarks had been directed toward Frankie and was in reference to an argument he and Frankie had earlier in the day.

The next day Frankie went to get Betty to go somewhere. When she got in Frankie's car she apologized to Betty for Forrester's behavior on the picnic. She told Betty not to worry about her safety because she planned to break up with him soon.

July encounters

One day Charles Davidson came home and told Maxine that he had seen Frankie at the post office, too far away for an opportunity to speak. He thinks she didn't even see him, adding that she looked disheveled, concerned, and not smiling.

Some of the waitresses at Cagle's Restaurant discussed that Frankie had recently shown up there with her hair in curlers and wearing a head scarf. This was out of character for Frankie, who was always very neat, tidy, and precise in her appearance.

It appeared she was slipping into depression, and no wonder. She was getting pressure from Gordon Forrester to marry, she had alienated some close relatives and friends by deceiving them, she had lawsuits pending with a mechanic and a car dealership, and her brother was demanding money.

She had commented, "I might just sell out and leave town."

She was serious enough to have sign painter Walter "Coffee" Hall make a for sale sign, with instructions to place it in front of her house clearly visible to motorists passing by on the Georgia Road.

She told him, "I'm selling out."

That sign was finished but still in his shop weeks later — due to unforeseen circumstances.

Sunday, July 21

Nat King Cole sang "Those Lazy, Hazy Days of Summer" and, "That Sunday, That Summer."

Well, "that Sunday" that summer morning Henry Rhode, a violin dealer from High Point, North Carolina, came to Frankie's antiques shop to discuss buying a violin she had advertised in *Hobbies - The Magazine for Collectors.*

The violin was made in 1791 in Germany by *Johannes Keffer with an Old English Bow,* and *guaranteed authentic.* Her advertised price was $600. (Keffer made another violin in 1791, which in 2016 in England was valued at $11,000 without a bow). She told Rhode the violin was not available, but took a $20 deposit on a banjo instead.

A 1791 Keffer violin available in 2016 in the UK price $11,000

She actually still had the violin, but out of view, being reluctant to sell it because of the dispute with her brother about it.

While Rhode was there at her house he met Forrester, who was in his sock feet wearing Bermuda shorts. Forrester told him he and Frankie were soon to be married.

Henry Rhode had visited Charlie Stanfield's shop the day before, on Saturday, after he had not found Frankie at her shop. So, he probably told Charlie that he came from High Point to purchase the violin from her. Charlie had not received full payment for it yet. There would be consequences if she sold that violin without fully paying him.

Soon after Rhode left, Forrester departed to return to Elizabeth City. He was expecting Frankie to join him there the next weekend so they could celebrate his 42nd birthday on Tuesday, July 30.

In the afternoon Frankie opened her antiques shop and that evening she wrote a letter to Gordon Forrester.

Sunday 8:30 PM   July 21, 1963   Postmarked
Monday 8 AM, July 22, 1963
Dear Gordon,

I miss you tonight. It was wonderful to see you this weekend. The day was quiet. I had several 'lookers' but the lady never came for the cut glass.
So goes business. Also, Mr. Tippett brought out some guy [Lewis Clayton] *from Detroit who wanted to take me out to dinner* [lunch]. *It was 2:30 PM and I was starved, but I said I had just had dinner* [lunch]. *What an accomplished liar I'm getting to be!*

I hope you are safe at home by now. I will worry until I hear.
I will write you again tomorrow. Right now I'm going

to wash my hair and then go mail this.
I love you darling,
 Frances   (Charles Davidson copy) SBI records

Monday, July 22
Frankie mails the letter to Gordon at 8 a.m. at the Franklin Post Office and later goes to lunch at Cagle's Restaurant with Lewis Clayton, the man from Detroit she met the day before, Sunday, at her shop.

Tuesday, July 23
Frankie dines again with Lewis Clayton at Cagle's Restaurant.

Wednesday, July 24
• At the White House, 16-year-old Bill Clinton meets President John F. Kennedy.

Frankie goes to dinner with Lewis Clayton at The Dillard House in Dillard, Georgia, and they make plans for dinner at his house with friends the next day, Thursday. [We learn in a later interview of a Mozart music concert at the Methodist Church].

That night Frankie phones Gordon Forrester and abruptly breaks off their engagement, marriage, and relationship, advising him he is no longer welcome at her house. The reason given is that she found out he had lied about some property he owned.

Thursday, July 25

Frankie writes another letter to Forrester in Elizabeth City, generally repeating what she had told him on the phone the night before, that she was ending their relationship. She sends it via air mail, apparently to make sure he got it as quickly as possible.

Dear Gordon,

I want you to know that your failure to mention your owning lots was of no real consequence, although I did wonder why. However, your flat denial of having them last night is an entirely different matter. I was willing to share my life and anything I might have with you. But I can tell you this, one-sided deals are out. I wouldn't marry you now for love or anything else. In short —you can go to hell!

No explanation or apologies at this point will matter. I think you know me well enough that you won't bother. I made you welcome as a guest in my home at the risk of my reputation, which I don't take lightly, but you are no longer welcome. In fact I never want to see you again.

Frances   (sent via air mail)

(Charles Davidson copy confirmed by SBI records)

Later Frankie has dinner, or possibly lunch, with Lewis Clayton and his friends from Ft. Myers, Florida at his house, and reportedly goes to a Mozart music concert at the Methodist Church. They make plans for a Saturday night dance in Dillard, located about fifteen miles south of her house.

Let's pause again for a moment while I reflect.

In writing Frankie's story, at this stage, I find it to be one of contradiction and confusion. She has painted herself into a corner, and the only way out is to sell out and leave town. That seems to be her plan — or is it?

She has made an all-out effort to get Forrester out of her life and already has begun a new relationship with another man with a much different personality.

Well, here is where the story gets back to where we started.

Chapter 16

Fatal Weekend

Friday, July 26

• President Kennedy announces a U.S.-Russia nuclear test ban.

For Frankie Bullock on this Friday, July 26 she had several things to do in the morning. In the afternoon between 1:30-2 p.m. she goes a few miles down the Georgia Road to Cagle's Restaurant for lunch. Her favorite waitress, who had served her and Lewis Clayton, was on duty and she was excited to know what she had thought of Lewis Clayton, the new man in her life.

Frankie had often talked with this waitress about personal matters, and her opinion was important to her. Frankie had told her about a man in Denver she used to date who had wanted to marry her. She also had talked about selling out and going to Colorado — or New Jersey. After lunch Frankie left between 2:30-2:45 p.m.

Frankie stopped by Charlie Stanfield's antiques shop on her way back home. He wasn't there, but she talked with his wife, Hazel Stanfield, for awhile. She told Hazel about breaking up with Forrester. Hazel and Charlie had once accompanied her to Elizabeth City to see him.

Hazel later recalled Frankie said, "He is no good, and I'm glad to get rid of him."

As she continued on her way home Frankie stopped by Susan Wallace's house to ask her boys to mow her lawn. They mowed about half of her lawn that afternoon, with plans to come back Saturday morning. Susan talked briefly with Frances, and helped one of the boys install Frankie's mailbox.

A mailbox? If Frankie was considering selling out, and had already requested a for sale sign put up, then why was she installing a mailbox? Maybe she had already made arrangements to cancel her post office box, get home-mail delivery, and to keep up appearances just let the process continue — so many contradictions.

Late in the afternoon Frankie went to her mother's home on Highlands Road. While there she told her mother she had broken up with Gordon Forrester. Her mother later said that she seemed calm, but still she had worried about her. She had suggested Frankie spend the night at her house. Frankie told her she might spend the night at a cousin's house, who her mother assumed might be Margie, not knowing they were both miffed.

Frankie left her mother's and passed by Margie's house; instead, she went to her friend Flora Ellis' home on White Oak Street in Franklin around 6 p.m. She pulled her car into the driveway where a nice blue Buick was parked that she recognized as the car driven by Flora's friend, Tom Johnson.

Ellis would later describe what Frances was wearing during that Friday visit.

She said, "Frances was wearing a blue and white striped dress and carrying a black patent leather handbag with a brown, bone handle."

Tom Johnson, 71, was a widower and well known in the town. He was a retired North Carolina Department of Transportation supervisor who had a nice home in East Franklin. When Frankie arrived they all made small talk. Frankie told Johnson that her car was making a noise in the rear end.

She asked, would he mind driving it around town to see if you can make out what it might be?

Sure, he was glad to, he told her. He drove it downtown and finally returned to White Oak Street. When he got back Frankie and Flora were eating supper. They had no cream for the coffee, so again he left them alone, and went to the Big Dollar grocery store in East Franklin to get a quart of milk. Frankie appeared to want to spend some time alone with Ellis and talk privately.

When Johnson returned they had coffee, sat and talked until about nine o'clock. While there Frankie talked to them about meeting a man, Lewis Clayton, and that she had been to his home to have dinner with him and some of his friends on Thursday. She thought he was a nice fellow and asked Flora to come meet him at her house on Saturday as they planned to go to a dance in Dillard.

During the visit Frankie told Flora Ellis about Gordon Forrester, that she had written him that she would not marry him — even if she had to leave town to get away from him. She added that she had met Forrester in Asheville several times. Flora had the impression Frankie feared him.

In other conversations with Ellis, she told her about a violin she bought from her brother Charlie, that he was not happy with the deal and might want it back. She also was going to stop loaning Charlie money. Frankie wanted her to read a letter from Forrester she had in her handbag; however, when she searched she did not have it with her.

She told them there was ironing to do at home, and started to leave around 9:30 p.m. As she left, Ellis gave her a small bag of onions. She was in a good mood, having informed several key people she had "dumped" Forester, thus easing her stress, and that she was somewhat excited that someone else was interested in seeing her — and was taking her to a dance the next evening, something new to look forward to.

Saturday, July 27

The next morning, after ten o'clock, as soon as the dew had burned off the grass, the twelve-year-old Wallace twins, Mack and Mike, took their lawn mowers down the street to Frances Bullock's house to finish mowing her lawn. Susan and her family always referred to her as "Frances".

It didn't take long with both of them operating a mower, with half already done the day before. When finished Mack Wallace knocked on the French patio door and — he got no answer. Frances' car was in the driveway. She almost always parked it in the basement garage. He knocked again — still there was no answer. The boys left and went home without collecting their money for mowing and installing the mailbox the day before.

The boys reported to their mother what had happened; that the car was parked in the driveway, she didn't come to the door when he knocked, so they didn't get paid. Mrs. Wallace wondered where she might be. She told the boys Frances would pay them later.

By that evening Susan was beginning to have some concern, and kept an eye out for traffic passing by her house toward the Bullock house. Later, in the twilight, she noticed that Frances' car was still parked where it was seen earlier Saturday morning, and something else — the only light she could see was in the bathroom area.

In the evening, Lewis Clayton, who Frankie had been seeing all week, drove up the new front driveway for their Saturday night dance date in Dillard, about fifteen miles south of Franklin. He saw her car parked in the driveway. He went to the door and knocked, but got no answer.

They were to be accompanied to the dance by the Terrell's, friends of his from Florida, whom Frankie had met at his home on Thursday when the four had dinner. So, he backed his car across the lawn, around the northeast side of the house, and parked among the trees, where it would be visible from both the front and back driveway, depending on which direction the Terrell's would take coming to the Bullock house.

When they arrived he explained that Frankie was not at home, and they should probably cancel their original plans. Anyway, he figured since he and Frankie had plans to attend the Methodist Church services the next day, on Sunday morning, she would explain what happened.

On Saturday evening, Gordon Forrester writes to Frankie in response to her "Dear John" letter he received earlier in the day:

Elizabeth City, NC   6:30 PM July 27, 1963
Dearest Frances,

What in the world has gone wrong? All I understand is that to the extent of your letter and why you didn't call? On Friday night [July 26 night of her murder] as you promised to do???? I cleaned on the apartment almost every night to have it ready for your arrival today. I was so much expecting your visit through my birthday [Tuesday July 30]. I played golf Friday evening (just putting) and got you a few more of those old antique nails but, that now seems in vain.

Honey, just what has gone wrong? You seemed in the best of spirits when you called Wednesday night [later he recanted this to officials].
Has some of that vicious gossip upset you? Something

certainly has. What is it? How in the world can you have thoughts about me holding out on you? I don't have any real estate anymore. Why don't you check with the register of deeds and you will find that to be true. You have always been with me in Franklin anyway. Honey, I've never told you any untruth. I've always been an "open book" with you & you should know it don't you?

Well, Doll, it's certainly a blue Saturday night without you, especially when I so expected you here through the 30th. Do you realize that I've spent the last four weekends with you, that we have missed on 2 or 3 since we went to Birmingham in April? What wonderful time we will have in the future.

I think my transfer will come thru by fall, although I've not heard anything. Anyway, this was you ---?--- for me to return to Franklin. It will be nice when we get married in the fall. I can hardly wait. Frances, please reappraise the situation. And write me or telephone me real soon, Please!

Today I did nothing much other than my Sat. routine such as go to the dry cleaners & post office. This morning's mail which included your "air mail" "Dear John" letter was enough to throw me for a loop. I've been blue ever since. (he appears to finish letter next day)*Today* [Sunday] *I'm playing golf with Mr. Krane & Mr. Lundell* [Pern A. Lundell ATF district officer]. *I love you dearly, please answer soon. Gordon*

(Charles Davidson copy) confirmed by SBI

Sunday, July 28

One of the first things Susan Wallace did on Sunday morning was to see if Frances' car was still in her driveway, and it was. Sometime later in the day, concerned, she and husband Ed Wallace walked out to Frankie's house. The car was still parked in the driveway as before. Ed noticed the windows were down so he rolled them up. It appeared she still was not at home. Susan showed Ed the mailbox that she and one of the boys had installed. At sunset, in the twilight, again Susan could see that light was still on and the car had not been moved. Susan's concern about Frances' well being grew more intense.

Monday, July 29

Being further east, dawn comes earlier in Elizabeth City than it does in Franklin. At 7:30 a.m., Forrester writes another letter.

Dear Frances,

Honey, it is certainly sad around here not hearing from you. <u>Really</u> Don't you think it a little foolish? to place much emphasis in a bunch of rumors that are not true? Please <u>reconsider</u>! Incidentally, Friday afternoon I got you 33 wood-carved old -   --?--- for $4.25 plus $5.00 for bird dogging them. What shall I do with them for the time being? I'll just keep them until I see you again. Tomorrow [July 30] is my birthday & I'm hoping for a surprise – like you calling up and saying you are at the apartment. I got a nice present (tie *clasp) from Geoff* [son]. *It's real nice. Marjorie* [2nd wife] *also would like the coffee & teapot to match the "Sheffield" that you are trying to sell for me. Well, love, I've got to turn too it's time to go to work. I love you, Gordon* (Charles Davidson copy) not confirmed by SBI

Early that Monday morning Susan Wallace was up before daylight to check to see if the Bullock house light was still on.

On my goodness it is, she thought to herself, and her car is still in the driveway.

Frances Bullock's 1962 Mercury Monterey
(J.P. Brady -SBI photo)

Susan Wallace had waited long enough, and was going to take matters into her own hands. Later in the morning Susan drove to Charlie Stanfield's shop, and told him about her concerns that something appeared wrong at Frances' house. She asked him to come and check it out. Charlie told Susan that there had been a man there this weekend, and she probably had gone off somewhere with him. Charlie did follow Susan back to Frankie's house, where he checked the doors and windows, and told Susan if Frankie had not returned, or was not heard from soon then he would come back and check some more. Susan also asked Charlie to enter the house by forcing a roll-out window on the front porch to enter that she knew he had done for Frances when she once could not get her key to work.

Of course Charlie was reluctant to do that because of the dispute with his sister over the violin payment. He told Susan that he would come back later, and now he was going to his shop. However, Susan noticed instead he went in the other direction and turned left on Womack Street.

It was later learned that Charlie had gone to the Howard residence on that street about 1:30 p.m. He had also been there on Saturday inquiring about some property not far from the Georgia state line, just south of the Mulberry Road, he was interested in buying. Mrs. Verna G. Howard owned 25 acres that Charlie was apparently was inquiring about, but he never talked with her, nor did he come back after that according to her nephew L.C. Howard, Jr.

Susan was aware of Frances' friendship with Flora Ellis and knew that she was a nurse. Susan called Ellis, asking her to come over and check on Frances. Ellis was getting ready to have lunch with a friend. She told Susan after lunch they would come over and check.

Chapter 17

Gruesome Discovery

Ellis shared Susan's concerns about Frances' whereabouts after trying to phone her several times on Saturday to set up a time to come over and meet Lewis Clayton. He was to take Frances to a dance Saturday evening. She was never able to reach her or to meet Clayton.

Flora Ellis and her friend, Tom Johnson, arrived at Frances Bullock's house after they had lunch on Monday, without any idea of what to expect. She and Tom got out of his car and walked past Frances' car in the driveway.

Ellis went up the steps to the back porch patio. The afternoon sun was high in the sky and shining brightly on that side of the house. Ellis cupped her hands around her eyes to peep through the French door window pane, but still it would have been difficult to see due a window covering on the inside of the door.

As she kept looking her worst fear was soon realized. She could barely make out a body in the shadow of the dining table. It could be her friend Frances Bullock sprawled on the floor.

She turned away and said, "Here she is Tom, beaten to death." Tom looked and said, "Yes, I see her."

A call was soon placed to the emergency dispatcher, Thelma Edwards, who immediately alerted both the police and the sheriff.

When the call came in, Sheriff Brice Rowland, who had been elected only six months earlier, was at his office at the Macon County Courthouse, meeting with one of his political supporters, Harold Corbin, a local radio announcer.

Upon hanging up the phone, Sheriff Rowland turned to Corbin and said, "There's been a murder — let's ride out there." Surprised by the invitation, Corbin quickly got in the sheriff's patrol car parked in front of the courthouse.

Years later Corbin told me, they sped down Main Street Franklin, onto the Georgia Road with the sheriff's car siren wailing and got there within minutes of the phone call. "It was quite a ride." Corbin added.

They arrived at the front of the Bullock house, quickly got out and saw a few people already there. The sheriff began asking questions of those present and those who soon arrived. Franklin Police Officer Ernie Wright was there, and he and the sheriff discussed the matter of jurisdiction, since it was barely inside the town limits. At that point the Franklin police apparently yielded to the sheriff's deparment to take the lead. Police Chief C.D. Baird was unavailable.

The sheriff found all the doors to the house locked. Deputy Sheriff Carroll Gregory arrived and was asked to try to see the body where Flora Ellis and Tom Johnson had indicated it was.

Gregory told me in a 2007 interview that he got up high enough at the door or dining room window and was finally able to confirm somebody lying there.

The coroner John Kusterer had been notified, and once he arrived he ordered the house sealed, allowing no entry.

At this point they apparently feel certain that the body is that of Frances Bullock and that she is dead.

The sheriff asked the dispatcher to summon the North Carolina SBI headquartered in nearby Haywood County.

It's been said that bad news travels fast, and news of the murder quickly spread around town even before the SBI arrived. My mother received a call from a neighbor who worked downtown, informing her of the tragic news.

She told her, "Frances Bullock has been beaten to death."

Upon learning the news; my mother phoned me about 2:30 p.m. at the A&P, where I worked, and we were in the midst of restocking shelves. The A&P then was located at the corner of Palmer and Phillips streets, which is today the Macon Printing building. A new A&P building was in the final stages of construction and opening at the current location of Ace Hardware between West Main and Palmer streets in Franklin.

When I answered the phone, she told me the news she had just heard, "Frankie has been beaten to death."

Of course I was stunned. This was almost unbelievable. I admired Frankie, and she had been spending so much time at our home she had endeared herself to us. I would learn later she had been stabbed.

Ebb Bullock's niece, Janett Gribble Blanton, was notified at her home that something awful had happened at Frankie's house. She quickly got her young son in the car and drove the short distance north on the Georgia Road to the Bullock house. When she arrived she saw a few people on the back porch patio and steps.

As she was getting out of her car, the coroner John Kusterer, whom she knew from the funeral home, rushed across the lawn to her.

In a conversation I had with Janett, she told me that the coroner told her, "You can't go in there, and you should get your young son away from this." She took his advice and left.

With word spreading fast and police vehicles visible at the house from the nearby busy Georgia Road and neighbor's houses, the scene quickly attracted onlookers with nothing to prevent them from coming onto the crime scene property and soon surrounding the house.

The crowd increased when the nearby Burlington Mills plant, a short distance down the road, had a shift change at 2:30-3:30 pm.

Back then there was no Franklin bypass, and Georgia Road was the main highway south to and from Franklin. Any of the employees of the Burlington Mills Franklin plant, or the Rug Factory in Rabun Gap, Georgia, taking that route in either direction would encounter slow-moving traffic, with cars parked near the house and along the sides of the highway. Many of these people stopped and were unabated walking up the sloping driveway or up the highway bank joining the ever-increasing crowd at the scene.

It was utter chaos and a nightmare for any outside forensic investigation around the house. It got worse when various authorities – newsmen and a few town dignitaries – were allowed inside the house. A local pharmacist and his employer were allowed in, both of whom lived on Golf View Drive across the street. The pharmacist later told his wife he wished he had not gone in because the victim's body was still in the discovered position, although respectfully covered.

Senior SBI Agent P.R. Kitchen in Waynesville was notified of the murder around 1:45 p.m. by the Macon County dispatcher shortly after the body was discovered, and he arrived one hour and ten minutes later at the Bullock house, around 3 p.m.

The first thing Agent Kitchen noticed was a large crowd of neighbors, officers, newsmen, a woman, coroner John Kusterer, Franklin police, an undertaker, and Macon County Sheriff Brice Rowland.

The sheriff met with Agent Kitchen after he exited his car and informed him that since the residence was just inside the Franklin town limits it was the Franklin Police Department's jurisdiction; however, the police had yielded to the Macon County Sheriff's department to take charge of the case investigation. Police officer Ernie Wright was present to confirm that. Chief of

Police C.D. Baird was out of town, but arrived later, and apparently concurred with the decision. Regardless, the main investigation was turned over to the SBI for support. The sheriff's department and the Franklin Police Department would counsel with the SBI and follow that agency's directives.

Macon County Coroner John Kusterer also spoke with the SBI agent, informing him that he had sealed the house once the body was spotted inside. Agent Kitchen then authorized the coroner to unseal the house and set out to find an entry point. Someone suggested they try a roll-out window on the front porch that was already open about three inches.

Once that window was pried open, Deputy Sheriff Carroll Gregory was instructed to go inside and unlock the doors. He did and then the investigators entered along with the coroner.

SBI front porch entry window
(R. Evans 2007 photo)

Frankie - A Life Cut Short

2007 dining room patio door on right
(R. Evans 2007 photos)

Once inside, they found the deceased, fully clothed body of 40-year-old Frances S. Bullock in the dining room, lying on her left side mostly on the hardwood oak floor and partially on a braided rug, with her back against the dining room table leg.

She was wearing a pink cotton casual house dress soaked in blood, mostly in the left chest area. Checking for wounds, they found she had been stabbed several times in her shoulder, chest and stomach area, later determined to be a total of six stab wounds and one defensive palm wound, as if she might have grabbed the weapon.

She was pronounced dead at the scene. Time of death would depend on a timeline of events, unless they found a witness — or the killer.

It was evident that an autopsy would be necessary. Coroner John Kusterer, who was also a mortician at the funeral home, notified pathologist Dr. Robert Boatwright, MD in Waynesville, requesting that he come to Franklin and conduct the autopsy, which would take place at Bryant Funeral Home later that day.

The victim's head was in a diagonal direction pointing southeast, toward the French door that opens to the back porch patio. Her feet and legs were in the opposite direction, toward the swinging door that led from the dining room to the kitchen.

A large amount of blood surrounded the torso on the hardwood oak floor and that area of the braided rug on which the dining table was sitting. Frankie's mother Odessa Stanfield had braided the rug.

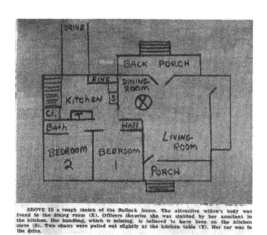

1963 Franklin Press - Bullock house layout

(2014 R. Evans sketch)

I later made a sketch from memory for forensic expert Dr. Max Noureddine for his analysis of the SBI photo we had viewed of the dining room after the victim was removed, showing the approximate pattern of blood on the floor and braided rug.

There was no evidence of forced entry into the house, suggesting she might have known the assailant and allowed entry to her home.

There were a few small blood spots on the oak floor toward the kitchen where they made a quick check, and more blood was found. It appeared that's where the attack had started.

An initial search around the kitchen was conducted for signs of a struggle and evidence. Blood splatter and castoff blood on the door frame inside the kitchen, and the nearby stove top further indicated the attack must have begun there.

There was evidence of an attempt to clean up. One of the blood spots on top of the stove had been wiped away and had already coagulated, leaving a thin ring of dry blood, which gave the investigators an idea of how long the assailant remained in the house before attempting to clean up. The clean-up appeared to have been abandoned.

The assailant left, locking all doors from inside, then by simply pulling the door shut when departing. It meant the assailant could not have re-entered, unless with a key or by forced entry of which they found no sign of that.

Two chairs were turned outward from a small kitchen table, indicating two people had been sitting there, then got up without placing the chairs back under the table. On the stove top there were stacks of bills, papers, and money order receipts. Nearby was the car key to her Mercury Monterey parked in the driveway.

When they checked her car there was a bag of onions on the car seat. They later learned the onions were given to her upon leaving Flora Ellis' house Friday night.

Left of the stove were two knives: a regular kitchen case knife, the other a longer bread knife. There were two tumbler drinking glasses. There was no sign of her black hand bag with brown bone handle that might have contained cash, an Alexandrite gem stone, and a ladies gold pendant watch, both she considered of high value.

(table & two chair location)   (sink - countertop - stove)

(kitchen doorway to dining room)
(R. Evans 2007 photos)

In the kitchen there was a small tray containing coins. There were blood stains in the kitchen sink. Under the sink was a jug of homemade wine.

The other rooms in the house were checked for more evidence. Drawers in a small table contained some letters from Gordon Forester she had saved. The disputed violin that she got from her brother was found, in its open case, in the bedroom.

A small trace of blood was found on the dress Flora Ellis would later accurately describe the victim was wearing at her house. It was lying on a bed where she had apparently changed into the pink casual dress.

Agent Kitchen instructed the available sheriff's deputies and police officers to look for other evidence and to make him aware of anything they thought suspicious.

Agent Kitchen had already selected reliable people he recognized from the crowd, and down on the highway to witnesses the crime scene. Two of these were Roy Guest and Frank Henry Sr. He asked them to follow him into the house, where they saw first-hand the gruesome sight that soon had Mr. Henry excusing himself to go outside to get a breath of fresh air. They were shown the body and toured the rest of the house. Guest needed to pick his wife up at work and asked to be excused from the witness list. Request granted.

Agent Kitchen then got the necessary equipment and items from his vehicle that he needed to process the crime scene for fingerprints and blood samples, and a camera to photograph the crime scene beginning with the victim, dining area, and the kitchen.

The two drinking glasses found at the kitchen sink, one with water and the other dry, were dusted for fingerprints. Neither yielded any latent, usable prints.

The only latent fingerprints found in the entire house, other than the victim's, was on the TV and on a door face. One belonged to her boy friend, Gordon Lee Forrester, who she had broken up with earlier in the week, and the other to her brother, Charlie Stanfield, who she had been arguing with about payment on a violin. Both had recently been in the house — often, and could have left prints at various times other than during the murder timeframe.

Once the Mercury car was processed for evidence it was driven into the basement garage to be stored as the investigation moved forward. The key to the vehicle was eventually turned over to the clerk of court for the estate disposition.

In the meantime, outside the crowd continued to grow. In a 2007 phone interview, Mack Wallace, who was only twelve in 1963, told me the only official he recognized then was policeman Ernie Wright.

Wallace said Wright came out and told the crowd behind the house to "Move back to the top of the driveway." "And we did," he said.

Franklin Police Patrol Officer Gene Ledford showed up downtown for his nightly patrol shift, but his partner with the patrol car was not there. He contacted the dispatcher, who told him they were at a murder scene at the Bullock house.

He went out there around 3:30-4 p.m. and saw the crowd outside with onlookers and reporters inside the house. By then some of crime scene had already been contaminated. He found a footprint near an outside window and went to the investigator to report it.

A few years ago in a long afternoon interview with Ledford at his home, the former, self-described "rookie" policeman told me the authorities that day had instructed him to go on his regular patrol of the town, and they would handle the crime scene investigation.

1963 Franklin Police Officer Gene Ledford
(police staff photo)

On the east side of the house were tire tracks in the grass that led from the front to an area in the back of the house among trees. They were later determined to have been made by Lewis Clayton's vehicle on Saturday.

Franklin Press photographer and reporter J.P. Brady was at the crime scene inside the house and was assisting the SBI with getting photos, which I've been told was a common practice in those days as the local news photographers usually had the better cameras.

Some local teenagers visiting next door came to join the crowd gathered in the back yard. Soon someone came out on the porch patio and asked everyone to move to the front yard of the house. They were preparing to remove the body from the house to the hearse parked in the back driveway. It would be taken to the funeral home for the autopsy soon to take place as soon as the pathologist, Dr. Boatwright, arrived.

As the investigation continued, someone pointed out the victim's brother, Charlie Stanfield, in the crowd. Agent Kitchen went out, approached him, and told him basically what had happened – that his sister had been found dead. He also told him he needed to talk to him about his sister's death. Stanfield said he needed to leave and go let his mother know, and he didn't know what she would think.

Okay, the agent then asked him to come back to the sheriff's office later in the day where they could talk in private. He agreed to come, but he did not show up at the appointed time.

Since he didn't show up, now it became imperative to find him — and bring him in. Authorities went first to his mother Odessa Stanfield's house seven miles east on the Highlands Road, where they found him and began to questioning him there in her front yard.

His uncle, Lloyd Estes, and wife, Donna, saw the commotion from their house on the hill and walked down to see what was going on. As they approached Odessa's house, they saw law officers and Charlie Stanfield in the front yard sitting in her metal glider chairs, talking.

The authorities informed all those gathered at Stanfield's house they needed an immediate family member to go to the funeral home to make a positive identification of the victim before they could conduct the autopsy, which was required by law. Estes decided he should stay with his nephew during his questioning by authorities.

Odessa Stanfield, her sister Nettie Hall, and Donna Estes then went to the funeral home. The coroner asked Odessa Stanfield to go in where her daughter's body was laid out to make the positive identification.

Sobbing she said, "I just can't do it."

Donna Estes said she would but was informed she didn't qualify as next of kin as required by law.

Evidently someone did make the official identification, and the autopsy began very soon after witnesses to the autopsy were quickly gathered.

It was important to proceed as soon as possible since the victim had apparently been dead for several days inside the house with no air conditioning during the hot July weather.

Ronald C. Evans

(staff photos)

1963 Macon Co. Sheriff   Franklin Police Chief
Brice Rowland   C.D. Baird

Charlie Stanfield's mother Odessa Stanfield
in her metal glider chair
(family photo)

Chapter 18

Autopsy

The official order for the autopsy was made by John H. Kusterer, coroner of Macon County, and conducted at Bryant Funeral Home in Franklin by Robert S. Boatwright, MD pathologist.

Required witnesses were listed as Kusterer, Bowden Dryman, and E.C. "Ernie" Wright. Additional witnesses, all male, were allowed after Mrs. Hermie Bryant Dryman, funeral home owner, assured them that what would be an invasive procedure to examine the nude body of a female would be conducted with complete respect during and after the procedure.

The date and time of the autopsy logged as: Monday, July 29, 1963 at 5:30 p.m.

Autopsy: *The victim Frances S. Bullock was noted as a middle age, white female, well nourished, clothed in a pink cotton dress with a partially torn Bobbie Brooks label, and undergarments (and Italian sandals). The wounds indicated she had been severely stabbed by a sharp instrument to the left shoulder and chest areas and lower abdomen any of which could have caused death and no determination of the order of which the wounds were inflicted. The dress was heavily soaked with blood in the left shoulder area. A chest wound delivered with such force the breast bone was fractured. The deepest wound had been delivered to the lower abdomen area. No major arteries were penetrated.*

It was also noted that the victim had a broken wrist possibly caused by her falling to the hardwood floor, and there was a questionable neck injury that after an X-ray showed no broken bones. In all there were six stab wounds to the body, most of which penetrated the dress, and one defensive wound in the palm of her hand suggesting she had grabbed at the weapon.

Also noted the victim's left lung was lacerated and there was evidence of a previous chest operation for removing the right lung resulting in a surgery scar on her back where the surgeon had gained access to the chest cavity.

In summary Dr. Boatwright believes, that death was because of multiple injuries by a sharp instrument.

Once the autopsy was completed, the body of Frances S. Bullock was turned over to the family and funeral home.

The clothing Frances Bullock was wearing, and other evidence, was cataloged and eventually sent to the North Carolina SBI Crime Lab for further forensic examination, mantaining a chain-of-custody throughout the entire process, according to protocol. The evidence was submitted by Senior Agent P.R. Kitchen to the crime lab on Oct. 5 and returned by registered mail Oct. 10, 1963 to Macon County Sheriff Brice Rowland.

Coroner's Inquest:

John H. Kusterer, Macon County Coroner ordered the Sheriff of Macon County on July 30, 1963 to forthwith a jury of six good and lawful persons (male or female), freeholders, and otherwise qualified to act as jurors, who are not related to the deceased victim Frances (Frankie) S. Bullock by blood or marriage, or to any person suspected of guilt in connection with the death of the deceased, to appear before the corner at Bryant Funeral Home - Franklin, NC on July 31, 1963 at 7:00 am, to view the body, take the oath, and adjourn to suitable place for the inquiry into the death of the deceased, as by law required

Once the jury oath was taken by the members and they were impaneled, the viewing took place at the funeral home on the day of the funeral; however, they postponed any decision until further investigation. Therefore the verdict was delivered at the inquest on August 9, 1963 at 7:30 p.m. at the Macon County Courthouse.

The verdict: That the deceased person Frances S. Bullock came to her death from stab wounds from a sharp instrument inflicted by person or persons unknown. Cause of death: Internal Hemorrhage. Signed by each of the jurors:

Ronald C. Evans

Harry E. Neal - (funeral home employee)
Bowden F. Dryman - (funeral director)
W.C. Burrell, Sr. - (car dealership and Mayor)
Edwin P. Healy - (manager of radio station)
Harold P. Corbin - (radio station employee)
J.P. Brady - (Franklin Press reporter-photographer)

Chapter 19

Looking for Suspects

Early on, investigators were confused about how such a brutal murder took place without much sign of a struggle. Everything seemed to be in place. The house was full of various antiques, cut glass items, stacks of dining plates of various sizes on the dining table, spinning wheels, and other antiques in the living room yet they were not disturbed. Despite the number of antiques crowding the living room, the house was immaculate.

There was no evidence that any antiques were taken, and some were quite valuable. The disputed German violin was found in the bedroom in its opened case. A .22 rifle and a shotgun were on the premises. The only item missing was the victim's black handbag that had a bone handle that had been described by Flora Ellis as what Frances was carrying when she left her house on Friday night around 9:30 p.m. It was suspected that the cut Alexandrite gem stone, an Elgin ladies pendant watch, and an unknown amount of cash were in the handbag.

Now that the crime scene was being investigated and the autopsy completed, the investigators were faced with the daunting task of finding suspects who might have reasons for murdering Frances S. Bullock.

Where to start first? Well, they already knew where

to start from information suggested by neighbors, family members, friends – and an informant.

They would start with that recently estranged boyfriend. Find him now, and find him fast.

Gordon Lee Forrester, a 41-year-old employee of the Internal Revenue Service stationed in Elizabeth City and formerly in Franklin, was their the highest priority person-of-interest, and the investigators wanted to immediately locate and talk with him. The same day the body of Frances Bullock was discovered, SBI Agent P.R. Kitchen sent word to SBI Agent O.L. "Lenny" Wise, stationed in Elizabeth City, to find and question Gordon Lee Forrester. Agent Wise located the subject and summoned him to the Elizabeth City police headquarters to meet with him and Chief of Police Bill Owens Sr.

In 2008 I spoke by phone with Bill Owens Jr., a North Carolina state legislator in Raleigh, who was a young teenager in 1963. He told me he used to hang around his father's office doing odd jobs of burning trash and out-of-date photos of car wrecks. He doubted that any of his late father's old records of such interviews would have been survived the many years since that event in 1963.

The meeting with Forrester took place around midnight on Monday July 29, 1963. Gordon Forrester was informed of the death of Frances Bullock.

They asked him to account for his location and

activities on Friday through Monday, July 26-29, 1963.

First off, he told them, "I was shocked by the breakup that occurred last week by phone and letter."

At another interview he gave them the letters, and after getting a special warrant for phone records, they confirmed a call placed from Bullock's phone to his phone in Elizabeth City on Wednesday, July 24, 1963.

He told them his alleged location for each of the dates and times. If true, he would not have the time to make the trip by car to Franklin to commit the murder and return to Elizabeth City. It appeared Forrester did have the motive, the means, but not the opportunity.

Since at this point they had no probable cause to arrest him, they released Forrester sometime after midnight while they went about checking his many alibis. It was now July 30, 1963 – Forrester's 42nd birthday, one that he had formerly planned to spend with Frances Bullock there in Elizabeth City.

In checking Forrester's alibis, there were witnesses placing him still in Elizabeth City at 7 p.m. Friday evening, July 26, 1963, and around 10 a.m. Saturday morning, July 27, 1963. However, that left 15 hours unaccounted for, a time period that he said he was alone elsewhere, or in his apartment for most of that time, sleeping or doing other activities where there were no witnesses.

Since a trip by car for the timeframe would not be very likely, other transportation by commercial or private plane was possible; however, checking

Piedmont Airlines passenger manifests and private commercial pilots did not yield any evidence he used them. The rental car agencies records at the Asheville airport were checked, and they had no record of Gordon Lee Forrester using their services.

The investigators went back to do a followup interview with Forrester, but he now had a lawyer who advised, if they were not prepared to arrest him then answer no more questions at that time, and he refused to take a polygraph test. Getting an attorney and refusing the lie detector test was his constitutional right; however, it unofficially raised a red flag for the investigators as a signal to continue to investigate him.

Forrester had been with Frances Bullock every weekend in July, including the previous weekend before her murder. He had been engaged to marry her, but she called it off three days before she was killed.

He was known to have a violent nature, especially when drinking. He was allegedly getting pain medication treatment [cortisone] for his back from Dr. Winstead, MD of Franklin, according to the doctor's nurse, Flora Ellis, Frankie's friend. Dr. Chase, a Franklin chiropractor, also treated Forrester for his back issue.

Forrester had been married three times. While living in Franklin, there were incidents when neighboring men, one a former highway patrolman, had to go to the Forrester home on Golf View Drive to subdue him and prevent him from harming his wife,

Marjorie, and their young son during his frequent drunken rages.

One of the neighbor's daughters phoned me a few years ago and told me that as a youngster she had been playmates with Forrester's son across the street, and had witnessed when her father had to intervene. She said Marjorie Forrester and her son spent the night at their house, and her father stayed all night at Gordon Forrester's rented house on Golf View Drive.

Forrester's reputation for domestic abuse became known to residents of the small town. His wife had been noticed around town, and at the First Baptist Church, with bruises indicative of such abuse; although no formal complaint, or restraining orders are on record. Former sheriff J. Harry Thomas admits he was made aware of the abuse but had no official request or authority to investigate.

Soon, divorce proceedings filed by Marjorie Forrester resulted in her getting custody of their young son with visitation rights for Forrester. She moved back to her home town of Ruston, Louisiana and was employed by Louisiana Tech located there. She married again and remained there with her son among family and friends. Her sister was especially helpful in caring for her son. In recent years I contacted Marjorie's sister by phone. The only comment she volunteered was, "Gordon was hard to get along with." Forrester would make occasional visits to see his son there in Ruston.

The SBI interviewed Jack Powell, who was one of Forrester's co-workers at the IRS Franklin office.

Asked if Powell thought Gordon Forrester was capable of committing the murder, he told them, "Forrester had a temper, and he was aware of his marital and drinking problems."

Powell years later told me that he had witnessed one of Forrester's outbursts while dealing with a person who had come to the IRS office seeking assistance. Powell added that Forrester was transferred to Elizabeth City in far eastern North Carolina, put on probation, and was instructed not to have direct contact with the public.

Powell and other agents had noted that Forrester seemed to relish extolling his power as an IRS agent, whether in an official capacity or simply in a restaurant having a meal or coffee.

I heard from several sources of an incident at a Franklin restaurant when Forrester became upset with a waitress for some reason that resulted in him throwing coffee at her.

During my research I did a telephone interview with Wayne Faulkner, Bullock's neighbor, who at the time was the accountant at Zickgraf Hardwood Co. in Franklin. He recalled Forrester approaching him at the post office. Forrester had told him, "I need to come and do an audit of your company records sometime."

Faulkner had replied, "Come on, the records will be available; however, he never came," Faulkner told me.

Faulkner continued that he later asked him, "I thought you were coming to audit our records?"

He said Forrester replied, "I found out what I needed elsewhere."

Investigators began checking Forrester's alibis with his supervisor John Ingram, manager of the Elizabeth City office of the IRS.

During the week in question Ingram said the last time he saw Forrester before the weekend was after work on Thursday, July 25, when he and Forrester stopped in at nearby Stock's Confectionary to have a beer. Ingram was not in the office on Friday and was on an official trip to Edenton that day. Ingram did confirm that Gordon Forrester had requested a transfer back to the mountains.

Office talk indicated Forrester had not been spending his weekends in Elizabeth City; rather, he was in Franklin with the "girl" he intended to marry.

On Friday, July 26, a co-worker at the Elizabeth City IRS office said that Forrester was in the office until around noon on Friday and then took off. Forrester said he was on an out-of-town trip on official business, but on the way realized he had left his files behind, so he canceled the trip and returned to Elizabeth City. Later that same day, he was at a golf practice range and ran into a couple of businessmen. One was John Fallman, a lumber company manager, who was having a tax audit problem and wanted to talk about it. The other man, Charles Gordon, a sheet metal business owner verified the conversation, date and time as accurate. Forrester had asked Fallman to come to the IRS office the following week, and they could discuss it. The two men left and last saw Forrester at the range around 7 p.m., Friday, July 26, the same time Frances Bullock was visiting Flora Ellis. The two men were interviewed separately by the SBI, and their accounts of Forrester's alibi were substantiated as comparatively accurate. Forrester's alibi for that time on that date was verified.

At 10 a.m. Saturday morning, July 27, Forrester was allegedly at Stock's Confectionary. Walter E. Comstock was sole owner and longtime operator of the business located near the IRS office in Elizabeth City, close to the waterfront. Comstock confirmed that, according to a waitress there, Forrester did come in on Saturday morning for a newspaper and a cup of coffee.

Comstock was later honored with the Order of the Long Leaf Pine, North Carolina's highest civilian award for his community and business service.

Walter E. Comstock

Before his death, I interviewed Comstock by phone on two occasions, and asked if he remembered Gordon Forrester. He said he did not, but did remember the IRS supervisor Ingram, SBI agent Lenny Wise, and ATF officer Pern Lundell. He told me he was sorry he could not be of more assistance.

The nearby Rochelle Cleaners clerk verified Forrester's alibi of picking up his laundry between 9-10 a.m. that Saturday morning, July 27. In recent years I spoke with the owner's daughter who is the current owner, and what she told me seems to support Forrester's alibi.

Forrester's friend and golf partner, ATF Officer P.A. "Pern" Lundell, confirmed that he spoke with Gordon about 3 p.m. Saturday afternoon, July 27, and set up a tee time for golf the next day. Lundell and Forrester played golf in Elizabeth City into the afternoon Sunday.

SBI Agent P.R. Kitchen still wanted to talk to Gordon Forrester. He went to Elizabeth City to meet with the local SBI agents Wise and Williams. When he arrived they contacted Forrester about an interview, and he told them he needed to get his lawyer's advice first. His attorney was out of town and could not be contacted. The investigators pressed that they really needed to do the interview — now. Agent Kitchen was needed back in Franklin to continue the investigation there.

Forrester, without his lawyer to advise him, invited

them to his apartment for the interview. When the three arrived he had already been drinking, and as the interview progressed he continued drinking until the process became counterproductive and was stopped.

They did garner some information that fit into the puzzle of his relationship with the victim Frances Bullock. He told them he had spent almost every weekend with her during the past few months. One time he flew from Raleigh to Asheville and met her there. He and Frances had done a lot of traveling, sometimes to antique shows. He said she carried large amounts of cash in her handbag when they traveled. He said that they made many trips out of town — at her expense.

When he would travel to Franklin or sometimes fly into Asheville to be with her, she would give him $100 to pay for the trip expenses. When they dined out she would slip some money under the table to pay the check for the meal and tip.

He volunteered that she had asked him to have the Alexandrite gem stone set into a yellow gold, Tiffany ring setting. He also told them about the Dear John letter and the love letter she had sent the week she was killed. He told them of her wild stories about her first husband being in the numbers game in New Jersey. She had talked about all the men, some of whom were married, back in Franklin who were flirting with her. He said he didn't believe any of it because she had a tendency to exaggerate.

When asked if he knew anyone who might have killed her, he told them he did not know of anyone; but when he was at her house she received several calls from a man — Pat Cable.

An SBI agent was assigned to check all Piedmont Airlines commercial and private airplane flight passenger manifests, and rental car agencies that Gordon Forrester could have taken to make the trip during the murder timeframe. His gas credit card was scrutinized for the period where he might have stopped for gas. All these checked out okay.

Agents checked with Elizabeth City jeweler Paul Bradshaw who confirmed Forrester had brought the Alexandrite gemstone to him for a ring setting. However, it was too expensive an item for him to get involved with and referred him to a jeweler in Norfolk for the setting. He did sell Forrester a wedding ring.

For the time being Forrester was cleared unless some new information was discovered.

Charles K. Stanfield was high on the list of persons-of-interest. He was the victim's brother, who also had demonstrated what was described as a "nervous type" with a violent temper if provoked. He had recently had serious arguments with Frankie about money.

Years earlier he had been medically discharged from the Army, where he had been hospitalized for a long period for mental illness.

He had been arrested in Franklin while on leave

from the Army when, after an encounter at a local Franklin café, he stormed out in a rage and stole a car, which he soon wrecked as he drove it on the Highlands Road east of Franklin. He was subsequently arrested and charged at his mother's home by North Carolina Highway Patrolman Clarence Byrd. The charges were eventually dropped by the district solicitor, with instructions that Stanfield immediately leave Franklin and report back to the Army.

Charles Stanfield was divorced from his first wife, Jean Dayton Stanfield, and authorities wanted to talk with her about her former husband. Arrangements were made, and they went to see her at home in Mt. Airy, Georgia.

When investigators arrived at her door she said, "I guess I know why you are here."

They were surprised by her greeting and quickly told her they wanted to talk about Frances Bullock's murder. She began sobbing and said, "I don't want to talk about that. I am out of that mess up there in Franklin." She added, "I am scared to death anyway."

When Jean Stanfield had heard of her former sister-in-law Frankie's murder, she commented that she had thought her former husband could have done it because of his abuse when they were married. She said it frightened her enough that he might come and harm her that she and her son moved in with her mother for awhile — for peace of mind.

Once the investigators got her composed, she told

them about marrying Charlie Stanfield in Clayton, Georgia in 1951 when her family was living in Macon County.

Before marrying him she had learned he had a nervous breakdown in the Army and had spent many months in a hospital for treatment of his mental problems. As for his mental condition in the marriage, she said, "Sometimes he could be as nice as anyone could be, and other times as mean as anyone could be."

She said they were married for nine years, and she still carries the marks of abuse he put on her during that time. They had lived in Franklin at her parent's home for awhile, then in Brevard, North Carolina for six years before moving to Georgia in 1956. They built a house in Georgia after cashing in some bonds to finance the efforts.

As far as she knows he didn't drink liquor. She admitted he had beaten her several times, usually about "silly little things," she told them. He was very jealous, and anything would set him off in a rage and he would not speak for days.

Jean Stanfield also told investigators that Charlie had told her that if she reported him he could avoid any charges against him because he had been in a mental institution while in the Army.

Jean Stanfield said that Charlie and his sister Frankie never really got along. If he asked her for money and she refused he would get mad. On one occasion when she refused him money he got angry and took some clothes that her husband Ebb had given him and threw them at Frankie, she said. In her opinion both Charlie and Frankie had mental issues.

She told investigators that Charlie just would not work and he relied on his pension from the Army. When they divorced a designated portion of it was to pay child support for their son. Charlie was bad to borrow money and not pay it back, she told them.

Grady Dayton, of Cornelia, Georgia, Charles Stanfield's former father-in-law, told investigators, he had been afraid something like this could happen.

When his daughter Jean and Charlie were first married they lived with the Dayton's in Franklin. He got to know Stanfield then, and knew he had a temper, and could go into a crazy rage. He didn't think he would kill someone — unless in one of those rages.

In July 1963, during the timeframe of the death of his sister, Charlie was living on Georgia Road south of the Bullock residence with his second wife and step-daughter. As a person-of-interest, authorities theorized his motive could be the continual arguing between him and his sister about refusing to loan or give him money, and more recently over a violin for which she still owed him the balance that she was refusing to pay him. None of their arguments over the years had led to physical violence as best they could determine.

Charlie Stanfield's initial interview took place informally in the front yard of his mother's home on Highlands Road. A formal interview took place the next day in the sheriff's office at the Macon County Courthouse on Tuesday, July 30, 1963, at 7:30 p.m., at the same time the visitation for Frances Bullock's family and friends was taking place down the street at Bryant Funeral Home. Family members were appalled that Charlie was being detained during such a somber occasion, but the authorities had good reason not to delay the investigation. The sooner they interviewed him the better.

Beforehand, SBI Agent P.R. Kitchen reports, "I notified Charles Stanfield of his constitutional rights, completely."

Whether or not he knew the consequences of answering Kitchen's questions without a lawyer present, Stanfield did not get an attorney, but that interview only produced minimum information.

On August 13, Sheriff Rowland and Agent P.R. Kitchen attempted to interview Stanfield again in the upstairs courtroom at the Macon County Courthouse, which proved very difficult. Still, he had no attorney.

It was revealed that Stanfield would calmly answer any trivial questions, but when they started touching on the arguments with his sister or pointed questions about her murder he became extremely emotional with loud talk, shouting, and crying outbursts. It became increasingly difficult to question him.

They did get an alibi for his whereabouts on Friday night, July 26 that he was with his wife Hazel at the Franklin Drive-In movie where the Walt Disney film

"Savage Sam" was showing. It was just the two of them for their daughter did not attend with them. He had no witnesses to verify they were there.

The movie started at 7:30-8 p.m., showing when it got dark enough, and would have ended at 10 p.m. or earlier, depending on what time it started and the length of the film being shown.

When they interviewed his wife, Hazel Sizemore Stanfield, she supported her husband's alibi.

They requested Charles Stanfield take a polygraph test, and he agreed he would. They also asked his wife Hazel if she would take the test, and she too agreed.

The two were released on their own to travel together to the Bryson City Highway Patrol office for the tests in two days on August 15, 1963.

Walt Disney "Savage Sam" (released June 1, 1963)
Friday night showing Franklin Drive-In (July 26, 1963)

Polygraph tests are not admissible as evidence in United State court trials. Before the tests can be administered, certain criteria as to the subject's emotional state and psychological profile also have to be considered. In some cases subjects simply don't qualify after they have been evaluated.

Whether Charles Stanfield's emotional state and previous mental issues would have disqualified him for the test is not known. In addition, it is not mandatory and is totally voluntary to take the test.

Regardless, the husband and wife traveled unescorted and without an attorney to the North Carolina Highway Patrol headquarters, in Bryson City, North Carolina. The tests were administered by SBI Special Agent John Vanderford and witnessed by Sheriff Brice Rowland and Sgt. T.A. Sandlin of the highway patrol.

Charles and Hazel Stanfield both failed the tests. The tests provided positive results of lying and deception for both subjects.

Because of the results of the tests, Sheriff Rowland and Sgt. Sandlin immediately interviewed the subjects at length with more pointed questions about the murder. Again the Stanfield's had no attorney. When pressed about the murder, Charles Stanfield, as he had done at the Macon County Courthouse, — began to holler, cry, yell, and talk so loud he could be heard outside the building.

When Hazel Stanfield was asked about the positive

results of the polygraph test, she told them the only time Charlie was out of her sight during the time of the murder was Saturday morning when he was out in the Coweeta community, and that he came back that afternoon appearing nervous and irritable.

Later information places him that Saturday, July 27, 1963 at the Howard residence on Womack Street, inquiring about some land he was interested in buying down near the Georgia line.

Agent P.R. Kitchen was not present at the Bryson City polygraph tests, but he did hope to talk to Stanfield at a later date.

In the meantime, there was an outstanding warrant for Charles Stanfield in Georgia for abandonment and unpaid child support, and until he had more evidence for probable cause in the murder, Sheriff Rowland had to avoid an arrest in Macon County that would make it difficult to get him back to Georgia for a trial there.

The District Solicitor Glenn Brown was being kept abreast of investigators findings in order to be prepared to go forward with a grand jury hearing. At this point that was not considered. Charles K. Stanfield remained a highly considered person-of-interest.

Lewis K. Clayton, age 54, a Michigan widower in Franklin for summer vacation, was next on the list of persons-of-interest. Frankie had only met him at her shop the previous Sunday soon after Gordon Forrester had departed her house on his return to Elizabeth City.

She was having dinner or lunch with Lewis Clayton almost every day since meeting him, and was scheduled to go to a dance with him on Saturday, then church on Sunday.

He had left a note for her on her door and tried to phone her when she failed to keep the dates on Saturday and Sunday, when it appeared she was not at home.

He had gone to Charlie Stanfield's shop; Odessa Stanfield's home, and elsewhere trying to find out about Frankie. He had also gone back to her house on Sunday to take her to church services, and he assumed she still was not at home.

A friend went back with him that afternoon to check on her, and to fill up a hole Clayton had cautioned her could endanger her customers. At that time Clayton left another note on a church bulletin.

When questioned by the SBI and sheriff, he had supportive alibis and volunteered to take a polygraph test if that would alleviate him from suspicion. They took him up on that, and assigned Deputy Carroll Gregory to take Clayton to the SBI office in Shelby, North Carolina, where SBI special agent John Vanderford conducted the test. Lewis Clayton passed with negative results of deception or lying. He was not questioned further.

Clayton was only a summer visitor in Franklin and was a resident of Detroit. He had been employed for 27 years with the Detroit Board of Education. His current job was a school Attendance Officer [truant officer] to investigate excessive school absences. He had a B.A. and M.A. degree, and a 29-year-old mentally challenged son, Douglas, who was with him in Franklin, but at other times his son resided in a special facility in Dearborn, Michigan.

I had recognized Clayton and his son as having shopped at the A&P in Franklin where I worked at that time.

In a story in the Franklin Press it indicated, *"Lewis K. Clayton said he accompanied her to a Mozart music concert at the Methodist Church on Thursday night and dropped her off at her home around 11 pm."*

On that Thursday in question the investigators have her at his home having dinner or lunch with him and his friends from Florida. It could be that they did both the dinner and concert.

Jesse Buford "J.B." Tippett, 39, a local used furniture dealer and upholsterer, was a person-of-interest due to a note he had left on Frankie's door, which she had apparently read and was later found in a trash can in her house.

He was a "finder" for Frankie's antiques business, which had caused some friction between the two due to him "running ahead" of her and making a purchase on one occasion. The note stated:

"I have been wanting to tell you something but afraid it will make you mad. You wouldn't believe it but it is

true, but I have not had a chance to tell you."

He claims he found a house full of antiques in the area of nearby Cashiers, owned by an elderly woman. He wanted to get Frankie in the car with him and go see the woman.

His alibi indicated he lived with his aunt on Rose Creek Road, and that he was at home during the murder timeframe.

N.C. Highway Patrolman Phil Gravely went to talk with his aunt, and she verified Tippett's alibi. His employee, Eddie Moses, later remembered Sheriff Brice Rowland coming to Tippett's shop located in an old store building west of the intersection of West Main and West Palmer streets. He said they had sat in the sheriff's car, and Tippett later told him they talked about the murder.

Patrick C."Pat" Cable, 44, was a person-of-interest. He had known Frances Bullock for up to fifteen years. They had dated maybe fifteen times in past two years, most recently three weeks earlier in June.

As for the time that Frankie was killed he was out of town on vacation. His alibi was verified. He told them he had never seen her intoxicated, although she did lightly drink alcohol on occasion.

Her personality, Cable described as having "a high imagination," and almost obsessed with talking about men who wanted to marry her: a general in the Army in New Orleans; John Peterson, a wealthy man in Denver;

and Gordon Forrester. He told them he would take a polygraph test if need be, but he was never asked to.

Johnny Bullock, Ebb Bullock's younger brother, a retired Army master sergeant, lived in New Orleans and was questioned because Frankie had him removed from the will where she and Ebb had bequeathed one-half their estate to him, in case they both were deceased, sharing it with her young nephew.

His alibi: He was at work during the time of the murder, which was verified by his supervisor at the U.S. Transport Terminal Command in New Orleans.

Johnny Bullock said he had given the inexpensive Alexandrite gemstone to Frankie that he had purchased when stationed in Panama. However, he did have an issue with her about his brother's watch that Ebb had left to him and she had declined to give it to him.

The director of the North Carolina SBI was making all the necessary contacts with local authorities out of state for interviews there and relaying the results back to Senior Agent P.R. Kitchen.

William W. "Bill" Townsend, Frankie's brother-in-law, was questioned as a person-of-interest since his ten-year-old son Paul was the sole heir to her estate when she had changed the will after Ebb died. At the time he and his family were living in Conway, Arkansas.

He had an alibi for the time the murder was committed: that he had worked at the Air Force base

Titan Missile complex until about 6:30 p.m., had dinner afterward at Coy's Restaurant, and after that played cards the rest of the night with several people he named. They were checked to support his claim, and they all verified his alibi.

Townsend told them the last time he had seen Frankie was in January or February of 1963 when Frankie visited them there in Conway.

William "Bill" Stark, Frankie's first husband, had been angry about their divorce settlement; however, he had not seen her since 1952. During the time of the murder he was at work at Roebling Foundry, a company that once made the suspension cables for the Brooklyn Bridge. His alibi checked out.

Betty Sue Guyer was Gordon Forrester's third wife, who he met when she was a waitress at a Franklin restaurant. She had known him for about seven years, and after his divorce they dated for only five weeks before they married February 3, 1962.

She and her young daughter went with him to live in Elizabeth City but only spent approximately six weeks with him, during which time his heavy drinking after work led to verbal and physically abusive behavior. He had cursed and thrown water on her daughter, who had medical issues since birth. Forrester ordered her to leave, and she obliged by getting a bus ticket back to Franklin for both her and the daughter.

At a later opportune time, her brother and a neighbor accompanied her back there to get her personal belongings, and she left her wedding and engagement rings on the table in his apartment. She did not see Forrester on the trip.

They were not officially divorced until April, 1963 through proceedings in Alabama mailed to her to sign and return, which she gladly did. She was glad to get rid of him, she told them.

She took an SBI polygraph test and passed with a negative result for deception or lying.

At the time she worked at the Burlington Mills plant in Franklin and passed by the Bullock house daily during the work week. She had seen Forrester's car there.

She had been divorced from Forrester a few months earlier and knew that he was currently seeing Frankie. She also knew he had dated Frankie before their marriage.

Investigators concluded that her willingness to cooperate and give information freely, take the polygraph test and pass, and her general calm behavior gave them no reason to suspect her for the time being.

Gene Bradley, a young man employed as an orderly at Angel Hospital, was questioned because he had been arrested by Franklin policemen Gene Ledford and Sonny Davis for brandishing a knife at Angel Hospital while intoxicated. He was released from jail after spending a night there, and once his knife was visually examined for blood evidence by the SBI, it was returned to Bradley.

He had no obvious motive or opportunity and was released.

While on patrol, Ledford and his partner Davis had reportedly seen him with someone else hitchhiking as it was beginning to rain near the Bullock home on the night of the murder.

Ed Wallace's statement to authorities appears to bring up a contradiction about the weather that night. He and his wife had gone to check on Frances Bullock during the weekend, and noticed her car windows were down so he rolled them up. This indicates it probably was not raining at the time when she came home Friday night around 10 p.m. and parked the car, with the widows down, outside the garage. That is how it had remained until the Wallaces came to check on her.

The SBI questioned Bradley as to his whereabouts on the night of Frances Bullock's murder. He said he had gone to Waynesville with a friend and his friend's sister, and when they returned they dropped him off at Angel Hospital, where he worked. He admitted that he often hitchhiked with another friend on the Georgia Road, but not that night. His alibi was verified.

The 1963 Franklin High School Laurel Leaf yearbook had him pictured in the freshman class and ready to enter his sophomore year that summer. His age possibly 15 or at most 16 years old, although the authorities' report entry lists him as 18 years old. The SBI agent commented at the time of Bradley's release, "he is just a kid."

Gene Bradley, freshman
1963 FHS Laurel Leaf yearbook

Gene Bradley later became an Army Vietnam War veteran. He died several years ago in Otto, North Carolina.

Chapter 20

Warrant issued - Camera Failure

A great number of other people were questioned in Franklin and elsewhere as various information came to them that might help put them on the path of any unknown person out there who could have the motive, opportunity, and the means to do the murder.

With all the leads, interviews, evidence, theories, and rumors of suspects that abounded, none of these had produced a real suspect to arrest or probable cause in order to get a search warrant to extend the search for forensic physical evidence that would link someone to the crime scene.

The only warrant was issued by Judge George Patton and Solicitor Glenn Brown in order for the SBI to check the long-distance phone records of Gordon Forrester and Frances Bullock.

The last long-distance phone call from the Bullock phone was placed on Wednesday July 24 to Gordon Forrester in Elizabeth City when she allegedly broke up with him. Other phone calls were to and from various places, some of which verified others' statements.

An unexpected glitch in the investigation came when they discovered the crime scene photos, taken the day the victim's body was discovered did not turn out. A number of reasons have been cited, mostly rumors about no film in the camera, a broken camera, or the rumor that it was done on purpose to protect some suspect. Regardless, they did not have any photos of the victim's body in place or of the crucial blood splatter and castoff blood in the kitchen.

Both the SBI and local Franklin Press photographer were supposedly taking photos that day; however, they did go back to the scene the next day, Tuesday July 30 to shoot photos of the blood evidence left where the body was lying, other scenes in and around the house, and in the basement. I have seen all those large black and white photos, and they are very good quality.

Steve Brady, son of Franklin Press photographer J.P. Brady, inherited his father's cameras. I spoke at length with Steve about his recollections of his father's involvement in the crime scene photos of the Bullock murder and about the cameras.

He was eleven years old at the time when his father came home after he had spent the afternoon and early evening photographing the crime scene and autopsy. His father wanted to shower and change clothes because the stench of the crime scene had permeated his clothing.

J.P. Brady went back to Franklin Press dark room to develop the photo film. Steve remembers some of the photos hanging in the dark room to dry, and being told by his father that he had taken all the photos of the crime scene, including the autopsy. He told me about his father's Nikon F 35mm camera that had an electronic flash he used at that time.

Steve said, "I used that same camera when I was employed as a Franklin Press photographer for a few years." He added, "There is no way that my father would have not known there was no film in the SLR camera, due to the way you have to advance the 36 exposure film."

"If there was no film it would take very little pressure to activate the handle that advanced the film, but with a full roll of 36 exposure film it took much more pressure."

He said his father was a professional, with numerous photography awards to his credits, and he also had a large Graflex "press camera" that used single 4x5 film packs preloaded in the dark room at the Press office and a flashbulb that each had to be changed after every photo. The film packs could have been empty and picked up by mistake in the rush to get to the crime scene.

Martha Duncan Rayside, who had witnessed J.P. Brady taking photos at the scene, describes it as a "large camera."

Her statement seemed to indicate it was the larger Graflex press camera that was used in the dining room crime scene on the day the body was discovered.

So, we may never know why the photos did not turn out that first day.

Ronald C. Evans

1960's Nikon F 35 mm (stock)

Graflex 4x5 Press Camera (Klaus photo)

Chapter 21

Neighbor interviews

Frances Bullock lived amidst some well known and important citizens of the town of Franklin.

<u>Wayne and Helen Faulkner</u> and children lived the closest, on the northeast side of her house. Frankie, who had no children, was elated when they had asked her one time to babysit with their little girl. She knew and got along very good with the Faulkner's.

When investigators asked them what they knew, and where they were the night of the murder; well, they could not have heard or seen anything because on Friday afternoon they had joined up with Bill Cansler's family to go and camp at Nantahala Lake, and did not return until Sunday afternoon. Their sons were in the boy scouts together.

When I spoke with Wayne Faulkner years later he basically told me the same thing. He told me that Frances had a couple of regular visitors after Ebb died. One worked for the post office and the other a tax man. He would see their cars there from time to time.

<u>Frank and Laura "Lottie" Duncan</u>, on the south side of the Bullock house was a wooded area, and beyond that the brick ranch style Duncan house with white trim. Near their house was a matching brick garage that had

an entertainment room, used primarily by their children, and a nearby brick outdoor grill and picnic table. Across a dirt road that ran behind their house was their barn and large pasture.

Frank Duncan was owner of the Franklin Lodge and Golf Course across the highway from their home. In addition, he had built the Franklin Motel on Palmer Street, was a board official of the Bank of Franklin, and owned the Palmer Street shopping center. They did not have a social relationship with Frances and Ebb Bullock. Lottie Duncan told investigators she had spoken with them over the years, but really did not know Frances.

On the night of the murder, Frank and Lottie Duncan were away from home and did not return until later that night.

They did not know anything was wrong until Monday afternoon, when Frank Duncan came home and told them that something was going on at the Bullock house with police cars. In a followup interview, Duncan told the investigators that their youngest daughter had information she had shared about a car speeding on the dirt road behind their house on the night in question.

Their two young teenage daughters were at home that night. The oldest was in the entertainment room section of the brick garage out back of the house, entertaining friends.

The younger daughter was in the kitchen, located

on the back side of the house, talking on the phone with a teenage girlfriend when she heard the commotion of a speeding car behind the house. She looked out the south kitchen window to see a light-colored car approach and exit south on Georgia Road. It was dark and she could not tell what make or model it was.

The SBI investigator himself drove his car down that dirt road from the Bullock house through a large mud puddle that required washing his vehicle afterward. He concluded that he thought it would have been difficult for a vehicle to speed through that without sustaining some damage to their vehicle. He would keep that in mind for future interviews with persons of interest.

Frank Duncan told them about a man from Asheville coming into their driveway by mistake, looking for Frances Bullock. She had bought furniture from him and her check had bounced. He was angry and trying to collect his money.

Duncan owned a barn and pasture behind his house, and he said once when he was walking his dog he saw Frances Bullock outside talking to a man in an older car. Lottie Duncan added she did not know Frances but heard cars at her home all hours of the night. When Ebb was alive they saw them often and were friendly with them.

The Duncan's oldest daughter, Barbara, my high school classmate, was apparently not at home during this time period. Only her two younger siblings.

Martha Duncan Rayside, the youngest daughter, came to me in 2014 at a funeral service in Franklin and wanted to talk about what she remembered about the Bullock murder.

She said, "No one ever talked to me about it, and I did know some things to talk about." I suggested we could talk later, and she agreed.

Martha D. Rayside's primary residence in 2014 was in West Palm Beach, Florida, but she owned a house on Golf View Drive in Franklin, where she was staying. She was in town for medical appointments in Asheville, visiting with her mother-in-law, and taking care of business with the Duncan house now vacant following the death of her mother and father.

I scheduled to meet her at 4:30 p.m. on October 28, 2014 in front of the vacant Duncan house. She had just had some tree specialists remove some extremely large oak limbs from the trees near the house in preparation for putting the house up for sale. We chatted briefly about mutual friends we had back in the 1960s while we made our way to a picnic table near an outdoor grill. We sat down at the table, and I asked her to tell me what she remembered about the events of the murder in 1963.

She told me, "I was fourteen years old at the time," and confirmed, "My parents were not at home that Friday night and came home later." She continued, "My sister Frances and her boyfriend were in the entertainment room attached to the garage playing records."

She said, "I was in the kitchen at the rear of the house on the phone with my girlfriend from school when all of a sudden I heard the loud noise of a car speeding down the dirt road that ran between our house and the barn and pasture we owned behind the house."

"I told my friend to hold on while I checked, and I ran to the south side window of the kitchen where, in the dark, I saw a light-colored car come to a stop at the Georgia Road and then turn left down the highway."

The interview provided another surprising bit of information the day that Frances Bullock's body was discovered next door. The sisters had known nothing about what had happened until their father came home in the early afternoon and announced that he saw something going on at the Bullock house with police cars and people there.

He had told her mother, "Do not to let the girls go up there," she said.

Well, some of her teenage friends soon showed up, and they were intent on going to see what was going on there.

"They invited me to go with them." Rayside said. "My sister was also invited but she declined, so I went with the group."

She stated, "When we got to the back of the Bullock house there were a lot of other people in the back yard. Someone came out on the back porch patio and asked everyone to move around to the front of the house."

"I had my little dog with me, and as soon as we got around to the front, he ran back around toward the back, and I followed to retrieve him." she said. "When I got back there they were taking a body out on a gurney to the awaiting hearse, put it in, and drove off."

After the hearse left, around 3:30 p.m., her friends and the crowd soon came back around to the back of the house. The French door at the porch patio had been left open, and we could see flashes of light coming from within. She said she was dared to go up and check it out. She slowly climbed up the steps to the porch and peered in, where she saw J.P. Brady with a large camera taking photos.

She told me that she asked, "Can I come in?" "If you want to." she told me he had replied. "So, I started in and saw all the blood on the floor, and I immediately backed out, and went quickly back down the steps." She added, "I was overwhelmed by what I saw — and never forgot."

At this point Rayside invited me to go walk with her on that road behind their house. It no longer continues onto the highway after they blocked it off when they made the highway four lanes in later years. It is also blocked off on Wallace Street between their property and the Bullock house. She mentioned that the road behind their house back then was regularly used by cattlemen on their way to and from the McCoy Livestock Auction barn located at the other end of

Wallace Street.

"I used to walk this way to and from school at Franklin Elementary and High School to avoid walking down the Georgia Road, where there were no sidewalks."

She remembered, "The Bullocks had a dog I was afraid of."

I told her, "That must have been King."

She replied, "I didn't know his name but I was afraid of him."

She invited me inside the house, which had been unoccupied and sealed up for awhile. We toured some of the rooms, and finally got to the kitchen area. She showed me where the phone was in the northwest corner and then walked across the kitchen to the window, where she peered out to spot the speeding car that night.

She told me, "On the evening of the day the body was discovered, we all got in my father's car, went downtown and parked outside the old courthouse. My father, Frank, went in to find out what was going on."

When he got back, he told us, "Frances Bullock had been stabbed to death."

"We were all stunned by this news — so stunned by it my sister Frances wouldn't go outside alone after dark."

During our three-hour conversation I had found Rayside to be genuine and open with her answers to questions, and her accounts of what she remembered from over fifty years ago were believable and accurate.

A week later I phoned her to clear up some questions, and she repeated her story almost exactly what I was told that afternoon. It corresponded to what her father had told the investigator back in 1963.

Annie Mae Higdon lived directly across Georgia Road on Golf View Drive in a two-story, white-columned house where Higdon, a registered nurse, resided after her second husband died. She was providing room and board for two Baylor University students that summer.

Higdon said she was awakened around midnight on the night of Frances Bullock's murder to what sounded to her like a woman moaning but could not tell from which direction it came. One of the student boarders had been out on a date and came in between 11 p.m. and midnight. He didn't hear or see anything out of the ordinary, he told the investigator.

Bob and Mary Lou Rollins, fairly new to Franklin, were renting the small house next door to Ann Higdon where Higdon's son, John, and his wife Dorothy Crawford had lived before they built their larger brick home just beyond the smaller house.

As Mary Lou Rollins recalls, she thinks it was the day she was painting an interior room of the house and had left the windows up to help ventilate the room.

Her husband, Bob, who was a North Carolina Agriculture Extension agent, had gone to a meeting in

Raleigh but was soon to return home later that night.

She had continued to paint well into the night, waiting for him to return. Sometime during the night, possibly around midnight, their dogs began to bark and she went to see what was going on but saw nothing. They did not know anything was wrong until Monday, when the body was discovered.

<u>John and Dorothy Crawford</u> were very well known in Franklin. He was a rural mail carrier and an Air Force reserve officer, and she was employed with the Macon County Social Service office. She later became the director.

In 2008, I interviewed the Crawford's in the living room of their home to find out what they might remember about the 1963 murder and the investigation. Soon afterward, they also were interviewed there in a WLOS-TV cold case report about the murder.

Dorothy Crawford told me she was never interviewed in 1963 by the SBI or the sheriff's office about the murder and wondered why not since she lived close by.

She knew SBI agent Kitchen, and saw him at a meeting and asked him, "Why didn't you come and ask me questions?" She said he told her he didn't think she knew anything.

She wouldn't, of course, since they were out of town; but still, she might've had other useful information, she commented.

She told me on that Friday night she was up late packing things in preparation to go on a trip to visit family in her Alabama hometown.

She said, "It was hot and we didn't have air conditioning." — "We still don't," John interjected.

Dorothy Crawford went on to say "the windows were up, and we didn't hear anything — nothing. Someone out there knows something."

Since they were out of town over much of the weekend, they did not know anything until Monday when it all begins to happen across the street. She then contacted Susan Wallace, who lived almost directly across from them. Susan filled Dorothy in on the events from Friday until the body was found.

Dorothy said she casually knew Frances, who had come to her house sometime after Ebb Bullock's death to return a casserole dish in which she had prepared food for the home during Ebb's funeral. She invited her in and they sat a chatted for awhile. Crawford implied Frances was an interesting person.

Susan and Ed Wallace It has already been established that Susan Wallace and Frances Bullock had become good friends. Susan's boys helped Frances doing chores, and they were friends with her nephew Paul.

Susan and Ed Wallace both were shaken by the tragedy that completely shattered the innocence of the neighborhood. Both suspected Frankie's brother had something to do with her murder due to his reactions at her house when told of his sister's death and his reluctance to go in the house earlier that day and check when urged by Susan Wallace to do so.

Their son, Dick Wallace, who was stationed in the military in Germany at the time of the murder, later lamented about the murder, telling of his mother's close relationship with Frances, who shared some of her problems with his mother.

On one occasion his mother had said Frances broke down sobbing. When she asked, "What's wrong?" she said, "I wish I could tell you Susan, but I can't."

The McCoys, Tommy McCoy and his wife, lived on past his family's livestock auction barn, where every Wednesday cattle auctions were conducted. His brother was the auctioneer.

McCoy knew who the Bullocks were but they were not close enough to really know them, and he knew nothing other than what was in the newspapers or the rumors about her murder.

Mrs. L.P. Gribble Compton, 75, lived between the Wallace and Bullock houses with her sister, Mrs. E.N. Evans. Their brother was Jack Gribble, who had a cabinet shop in Franklin. He had suggested to the investigator they should talk to them.

Mrs. Compton was alone the night of the murder as her sister was in the hospital in Sylva. She said she did not hear or see anything suspcious that night.

Ronald C. Evans

Chapter 22

Other interviews

<u>Jimmie Stanfield</u> was Frankie Bullock's first cousin. His father, David Stanfield, was the youngest in his family, and Frankie's father Grover the oldest. Jimmie and his wife, Willene Moses Stanfield, both worked at the Burlington Mills plant. She worked the day shift and he worked the night shift.

Sometimes he would stop by and visit with his cousin Frankie sitting on the back porch patio chatting. She had told her cousin Margie about Jimmie's visits. The visits were casual while waiting for time for him to go to work a short distance down Georgia Road to the plant.

Their Aunt Mae Stanfield did some babysitting for them and she often took their young daughter with her to visit Frankie. Willene told me she recalled on one visit Frankie ran the bathroom tub with water and allowed her little girl to get in and play while Frankie and Aunt Mae chatted.

The investigators interviewed Jimmie Stanfield for any knowledge he might have that would provide information for the investigation. He was at work on the Friday night shift at the Burlington Mills plant July 26, 1963. He knew nothing about the murder until on his way to work on Monday July 29, 1963, the day her body was found. He stopped and joined the crowd of onlookers at the scene.

Jimmie remained calm during the entire interview, investigators noted.

Jimmie Stanfield told them that Frankie had told him about a wreck near the Holiday Inn in Asheville involving a drunk driver of a telephone truck. The guy had paid her $200 for damages in order not to report it.

Investigators found no record of a check being deposited in her account, or the accident, so she could have received cash from the man, or simply cashed the check.

Dr. Hilton Seals, MD of Sylva, Frances S. Bullock's doctor, was interviewed and he informed the investigator that his patient was afraid to take medicine and even hesitated to take what he prescribed. He saw her for the last time May 22, 1963. She had casually mentioned her plans for marriage to Gordon Forrester and talked a lot about him.

Sometime after that, on a Saturday night, he received a phone call from Washington, DC from Gordon Forrester. Dr. Seals was also an ordained Baptist minister, and Forrester told the doctor that he [Dr. Seals] was supposed to marry the couple on the following day, and he had called to tell him the wedding was off for now.

He told the doctor that Frances had sent him a telegram stating she had to go an Atlanta hospital for surgery.

Dr. Seals told investigators that Bullock had never said anything to him about performing a wedding ceremony for them that she had only talked of a possible marriage. He added that the caller appeared to be intoxicated and that Forrester abruptly hung up his phone. Dr. Seals was not aware of any pending operation she was to have in Atlanta.

Tex Corbin, a high school friend, told me of meeting Frances Bullock. He was in the Army and had a disabling accident for which he had been hospitalized for a long duration at Walter Reed Hospital in Washington, DC.

In May, 1963 he had been returning to Franklin from Washington by bus that was on its way to Bryson City, North Carolina. He decided to get off in Dillsboro and try his luck at hitchhiking the rest of the way to Franklin. A light colored Mercury car driven by Frances Bullock and passenger, her mother, stopped and gave him a ride to downtown Franklin, he said. They had told they were returning to Franklin from a doctor's appointment

That happened in the spring before Bullock's murder, he told me. That's the only encounter he ever had with her, and he was shocked by the news of her murder. He had not known of her father's military service in France during World War I or of his death at the VA hospital, which might have compelled Frances to stop that day.

<u>Joe M. Henry</u>, rock and gem shop operator, said he had known Frankie Bullock most of her life. She had brought him an Alexandrite stone to examine. "About the size of the tip of my little finger" he told them. The gemstone was later described as "dime size". She had thought it was worth $7,000 and had sent it to Tiffany's for appraisal. Their evaluation revealed it was imperfectly cut and worth only $600.

Henry said he had seen her recently riding with a man he did not recognize. She was sitting over very close to him.

<u>J. Harry Thomas</u>, former Macon County sheriff, said he barely knew Frances Bullock, but he knew Ebb Bullock and had been in the Lions Club with him.

When he was sheriff he had received complaints about Gordon Forrester's reputation of violence when he was drinking and thought he could be a very good suspect.

He said he had arrested Charles Stanfield on a warrant from Clarksville, Georgia, where his former wife, Jean Stanfield, had him indicted for abandonment and non-support of her and their son.Thomas said Charles made light of it, that he didn't have time to come in and make bond. The former sheriff said he almost had to force him to make bond. Thomas didn't know what happened in the case because he left office, and the jurisdiction fell to the current sheriff, Brice Rowland.

Investigators checked the local and state court records, and other agencies for court cases or arrest records of the major persons-of-interest. Charles Stanfield's child non-support and abandonment was all they found.

J.P. Brady, Franklin Press reporter-photographer, commented about Marjorie Forrester's husband's abusive treatment of her. Also he talked about Frances Bullock's very hysterical, unreasonable behavior at a car wreck scene he was covering for the Press. He said she "took a fit" and "raised Cain" with a person who had just ridden out to the scene with him.

Willie Mae "Bitsy" Gribble [Reed], Frankie Bullock's sister-in-law, said she had heard her brother, Ebb Bullock, say he was going to have to stop loaning money to his brother-in-law, Charlie Stanfield. He was forever demanding that Ebb give him money.

Frankie had told her that Charlie would find out where she had a charge account, go there and make personal purchases then charge to her account. They were constantly in some kind of fuss, but never came to blows — that she knows of. She said both had rather hot tempers. She said that Frankie tried to sell her ladies Elgin pendant watch, a family heirloom, for about a year — and it was now missing.

Charles Davidson operated a well drilling business and

was Frankie's first cousin. His mother was Frankie's aunt Minnie Stanfield Davidson, who had been kind to Frankie during her younger years. Charles had been a close friend of Frankie's husband, Ebb Bullock.

On one occasion Ebb had asked him to accompany Charlie Stanfield to Mt. Airy, Georgia where he was to have a meeting with his ex-wife, Jean Stanfield, about child support payments. Ebb Bullock was concerned, knowing of Charlie Stanfield's spousal abuse during the tumultuous marriage with Jean Stanfield, he might try to harm her.

Ebb also was aware that Charles Davidson when in service had worked as an orderly in an Army hospital that treated patients with mental issues, and that he would know how best to control a volatile situation should it arise.

Ebb told him, "Don't let him out of your sight."

Davidson accompanied his cousin, Charlie Stanfield, to and from Mt. Airy, Georgia and there were no incidents where he had to intervene.

Charlie Stanfield had shown Charles Davidson the German violin and told him he had been offered a lot of money for it.

Davidson had a well-known fascination with science, history, and unexplained phenomenon, subjects that came up in conversations he had with almost anyone.

Upon Frankie's death he immediately began forming a hypothesis about the murder.

He shadowed the investigators, giving information to them about Frankie's family connections, all the while gaining information from them about the investigation.

During a week night after Frankie's body was discovered, the family gathered at Odessa Stanfield's house. There, Charles Davidson told me, he was considering driving to and from Elizabeth City to prove he could do it in the allotted timeframe of the murder. It is not known if he actually did attempt the drive. He doggedly pursued the case for many years.

Some of his suggestions seemed viable others not so, and on some occasions the sheriff invited him to ride with him and see if they panned out. Most hit a dead end. During those associations with the sheriff he gained first-hand knowledge about the investigation.

Davidson had removed a kitchen knife from the Bullock kitchen utensil drawer. It had a six-inch blade, about the size he thought could have caused the fatal wounds, and brought it to the sheriff's attention and requested they check it for blood evidence.

Note: Evidence obtained at a crime scene has a chain-of-custody protocol to be maintained; otherwise, it can be challenged in court. A duly sworn officer of the law must retrieve, or witnesses the retrieval of the evidence, and present it to the next authority, including sending it to a crime lab and back.

This was a gray area with this knife since Charles Davidson had shown he could be trusted and had contributed much family information, so they allowed it to be entered in the testing phase of the evidence. After all, he was around them on a regular basis watching from afar.

The knife was tested by the SBI Crime Lab along with the bloody dress, undergarments, sandals, a stained wash cloth, and a soiled blue sweater. There was no blood evidence found on the knife, and it and all the other evidence remains in the custody of the Macon County Sheriff's Office today after more than fifty years.

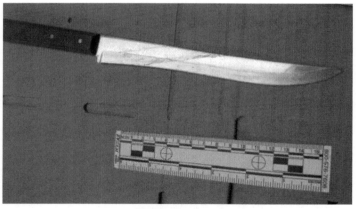

(R. Evans photo)
Six inch kitchen knife submitted by Charles Davidson

Davidson was also an amateur artist, good with pencil portraits and sketches. Once, while visiting at our house he had my sister Judy sit for a pencil drawing, and I recall it was pretty good.

The SBI showed Davidson the Alexandrite gemstone they had retrieved from Gordon Forrester. It was supposed to be the one Frankie had shown Davidson. He examined it under a high-power glass and told them it was not the same stone.

He volunteered a sketch of what he remembers being shown – rectangular in shape, displaying eight facets, and with an uneven cut. They entered his sketch into their records, and Faye Wells and I were shown the sketch during our later Q&A session with the SBI attorney. Davidson had told them it changed color from reddish purple to green depending on the light. The imperfect cut had been verified by a Tiffany Company evaluation when Frankie sent it there. Her niece Faye Wells now has the gemstone and it was recently professionally evaluated to be synthetic.

<u>Franklin Police Officer Ernie Wright</u> had found the stained washcloth and soiled blue sweater in the basement of the Bullock house and submitted them to the SBI for forensic testing. No conclusion about the washcloth stain or about soiled sweater was reached until 2014, when modern forensic chemicals determined the washcloth stain was blood. The soiled sweater tested negative for blood.

Wright reportedly formed his own theory about the murder, but was never able to substantiate it.

<u>Margie Stanfield Evans</u> was another of Frankie's first cousins, and a friend, who had helped her during the period following Ebb's death. Frankie visited her

regularly.

Frankie had shown her the pendant watch that was a family heirloom of Bitsy Gribble's.

Frankie had shown my brother, Tommy, the gemstone(s), wrapped in tissue that she carried in her hand bag along with the watch. Margie recalls she had two similar gemstones but was not sure both were Alexandrite.

Tommy Evans was a gifted artist who could appreciate the items she often displayed to him. She gave him an intricate carving of six elephants that had belonged to Ebb and was later passed on to me. It is either ivory or some other material; regardless, I treasure it.

Elephant carving

The investigators had come upon a pendant watch fitting the family's description. It supposedly was found under the gym bleachers at the high school.

A watch trader, who hung around the McCoy livestock auction building not far from the Bullock house, said he got it from a young man who found it.

In a full-out effort to identify the watch, the investigators took it to Jamison Jewelers in Franklin, and other key people who had seen the watch that was a Bullock family heirloom.

They probably would have first shown this watch to Willie Mae "Bitsy" Gribble [Reed], who had inherited her watch from her mother, and it was that watch that was in question. They might have shown to Bitsy's daughter, Janett Gribble Blanton, who years later described to me the watch that her grandmother, Sudie Bullock Pinson, had owned. Bitsy had given it to Frankie on consignment to sell at her antiques shop.

Agent Kitchen and Sheriff Rowland went to Margie's house and asked if she recognized it. She examined it and wasn't sure. She told them she knew the one Frankie had shown her was an Elgin because her youngest daughter had a Bulova watch at the time, and she and Frankie had teased each other about which was the better brand.

The investigators continued with a few questions Margie might be able to answer. Frankie had told her about how her brother Charlie always wanted money, and that she was going to quit giving him any. She told about Charlie and Ebb having trouble over money, but didn't recall the details.

Frankie had told her that she did not want to appoint her mother, Odessa, the administrator of her will, concerned that Charlie might take advantage.

Bill Townsend, Odessa's son-in-law, had stayed

behind in Franklin after Frankie's funeral until he knew who would be named administrator, perhaps for that same reason. He had to be concerned since his ten-year-old son Paul was the sole heir of Frankie's estate.

Chapter 23

The Funeral and the Will

The funeral for Frances Stanfield Bullock was to take place on Wednesday, two days after she was found dead in her home.

Her oldest sister, Nettie Mae Lear, lived in Burlington, New Jersey and was traveling south by train with her eight-year-old daughter, Faye. Her youngest sister, Doris Townsend, was in Conway, Arkansas and would be traveling east with her husband and children.

Faye Lear Wells, Nettie Mae's daughter, recalls the phone call to their home in Burlington, New Jersey when she was just 8 years old. She answered the call, and the person [Lloyd Estes] on the other end asked to speak to her mother. Her mother answered and was given the tragic news of her sister's death.

Faye told me, "My mother practically collapsed, and I ran to the dairy barn and got my father. The next thing I remember we were on a train headed to North Carolina." She added that "Frankie's tragic and unexpected death completely devastated my mother and the family."

Final funeral arrangements were made with the plans for the visitation for family and friends on Tuesday evening July 30, 1963 at Bryant Funeral Home in Franklin, the day after the discovery of

Frankie's body.

Services were held the following day at 11 a.m. on Wednesday July 31, 1963 at the First Methodist Church, across the street from the funeral home, conducted by the pastor Rev. J.P. Hornbuckle Jr., and the Rev. Fred Sorrells. Pallbearers were Mack, Theron, and Leo Stanfield; Tommy and Ronnie Evans; and Charles Davidson. Burial was beside her husband Ebion "Ebb" Bullock on the far hillside overlooking Woodlawn Cemetery in Franklin.

I recall we met with the family at the funeral home, and afterward we all walked across the street for the ceremony. I remember there wasn't an overflowing gathering at the church, mostly family and friends. Being a murdered widow's funeral, I suppose I expected more. It was not the turnout I had seen at Ebb's funeral.

As for the service itself, I don't recall that much, except for Rev. Hornbuckle's remarks about Frances Bullock's knowledge of antiques, how she could feel the texture of a piece of cut glass and determine its worth. He effectively went through the motion of having an imaginary piece held high in the palm of his left hand while slowly and lightly rubbing it with the fingers of his right hand.

This was my brother Tommy and my first occasion to be funeral pallbearers, and it was a somber one.

Before the immediate family was to leave and return to their respective homes, there was the matter of

Frankie's will.

Who was to be appointed administrator of the will and would handle the legal matters concerning the estate through the Macon County Clerk of Court?

The clerk, Winton Perry, had to issue an order to break open the safety deposit box because they could not find the key. The key could have been in Frankie's handbag that was missing.

The will stipulated that Frankie's sister, Mrs. Robert A."Nettie Mae" Lear, was to be administrator. The sole heir to the estate named in the will was Paul Townsend, the 10-year-old son of Frankie's sister Doris and Bill Townsend. The estate was put into a trust also administered by Nettie Mae Lear and would be totally Paul's when he was 25 years old. There were provisions for certain exceptions – for his education, medical emergencies, and some left to the trustee's discretion.

Paul Townsend, ten-year-old heir to Frances Bullock's estate

Ronald C. Evans

Rumors

Meanwhile, the investigation continued as rumors of suspects multiplied with each passing week.

By the end of summer 1963 Franklin, had lost some of its innocence. Residents locked their doors for fear a killer was among them, and as summer moved into fall no arrest or new information did little to ease their concerns.

Within a couple of months of Frances Bullock's murder there were no new updates from any of the investigating agencies to report in the newspapers.

With no new official information, community gossip fueled ideas of who could have done the crime. That gave rise to several rumored suspects and theories. Some of these rumors gradually began to be told and believed as the truth, depending on which was the favorite rumor.

This was quite unfair to the innocent persons whose names surfaced and equally unfair to the families of those persons.

In my research I found that the investigators all along knew exactly the persons-of-interest to focus on, and diligently investigated them; however, they did spend a good bit of time on the rumors just in case they might gain new information by "shaking the tree to see what falls out."

I hesitate to write about or glamorize any of those rumors I have heard over the years, preferring to follow the science and proven investigative techniques as the more reliable course for the facts — just the facts.

Anything else only produces sensational, fictional entertainment with disregard for the truth. The old humorist theory comes to mind of "not letting the truth stand in the way of a good story." Well, this story is worth telling — as the truth.

I have been privy to official information in several sessions with the SBI and at the sheriff's office and detention center, where I took detailed notes and at times tape recorded information about the original investigation. Combined with other information I discovered on my own, and from more recent forensic investigations I personally discount the typical rumors I've heard from 1963 to present day.

Were there other persons out there who could have committed the murder? Maybe strangers, vagrants, or hitchhikers from the highway who randomly chose her as a victim? Possibly, but the recorded facts seem to dispel these theories, and for important reasons.

Authorities remain convinced that, whoever was the killer, it appeared to have been someone she knew, someone who was allowed in her house with no sign of forced entry.

Other facts include: She had not taken time to park her car in the basement garage after arriving home from a visit with Flora Ellis and her friend sometime past

9:30 p.m.

There was a bag of onions Ellis had given her still on the car seat; and the car windows were rolled down — none of this her usual routine.

She had taken time to change clothes after arriving home. Perhaps, after changing clothes, she had planned to return to move the car and remove the onions and someone came to visit – or somone was already there when she arrived. We can't know for sure; regardless, it really appeared it was someone she knew based on the scene.

The attack occurred in the confines of her kitchen, where it appeared two people had been seated having a conversation. In all likelihood a disagreement got out of hand, leading to an attack with possibly an available weapon already there in the kitchen.

Robbery seemed not to be the motive due to the valuable antiques and German violin not taken. Perhaps there was something in her black handbag the person wanted, or wanted to make it appear to be a robbery? It was the only item confirmed missing in the household and antiques shop. The key to the car was left on the counter and the car in the driveway. Those are facts, with some conjecture on my part.

With 20/20 hindsight there are some things that are still troubling about the case. There was never any kind of reward offered by the SBI, the sheriff's office, or the family as an incentive for information leading to an arrest and conviction of a possible suspect. I have often wondered — why not? I am not aware if a reward was ever considered or discussed.

Something else I have wondered about; were fingernail scrapings taken from underneath each of the victim's fingernails? I can find no record of that procedure, which was standard in many homicide investigations in 1963. Of course these days that would be valuable evidence for DNA testing.

I am still puzzled why one of the main persons-of-interest, Charles Stanfield, never retained or sought advice from an attorney given the extreme questioning and scrutiny he and his wife were subjected to. He was advised of his constitutional rights to do so.

On the other hand the other top person-of-interest, Gordon Lee Forrester, immediately retained a lawyer and refused a polygraph test.

Neither Stanfield nor Forrester were ever charged or named as "official suspects"; nor was anyone else for that matter.

Otherwise, aside from the lack of local experience, lack of crowd control, plus the loss of crucial photos at the crime scene, it appears the authorities did the best they could when considering the investigative techniques, technology, resources, and manpower available to them in 1963.

Chapter 25

Cold Case investigation

The 1963 North Carolina SBI Director Anderson sent copies of the crime scene photos to the district solicitor and Macon County Sheriff Brice Rowland.

In 1987 SBI Agent Charles Hess II requested the Frances Bullock murder evidence, then in the possession of Franklin Police Chief Ernie Wright. It was part of a five-year cold case project the N.C. SBI created and dubbed MUST (Murder Unsolved Team).

Becky Boring, who had worked in the old Franklin town office for many years, had told me she had seen the Bullock dress stored at the office.

When former agent Hess was contacted after he retired and I asked about the evidence, Hess told me nothing was ever done with the evidence. He returned it to the Franklin Police Department. When Police Chief Terry Bradley was contacted he told me they did not have it but that he had assisted agent Hess.

One year later, when I inquired again about the evidence,

Chief Bradley told me, "I have good news, we found it." "When was it found?" I asked. "About a year ago," he answered.

"Was that after I first called asking about it?" I continued.

"Yes, soon after that," he stated.

Yes, this was good news. He had found it in the Franklin Police evidence room after being contacted by the sheriff's office. Since the Franklin police had originally yielded to the sheriff to lead the investigation, he turned the evidence over to them — but not before he did an inventory. They signed for it when picking it up.

He read the inventory list to me over the phone, and it completely matched the inventory the 1963 SBI crime lab had sent back to Sheriff Rowland by registered mail October 10, 1963. We had been shown that list during our Q&A session with the SBI attorney John Watters.

The evidence had ended up in the Franklin Police Department custody, apparently requested by Chief Ernie Wright who had participated in the original murder investigation that had become a cold case.

For further information I contacted former Macon County sheriffs.

Hubert Bateman had served as a deputy in the second term of Rowland and said they had nothing new to go on even then, and nothing during his terms in office.

George Moses, who served two separate terms, said it was a cold case and he never did anything with it.

Homer Holbrooks said much the same thing. Holbrooks did refer me to former policeman Gene Ledford for information he might have from the original investigation.

In 1991 SBI Agent Charles Moody took the Frances Bullock case file to the FBI National Academy training course at Quantico, Virginia. Each agent attending the course was requested to bring a case of interest to the event as a class project conducted by experienced FBI personnel. As it turned out, the Frances S. Bullock murder case was chosen and profiled.

From that point Moody maintained an interest in the case as he rose in the ranks of the SBI to agent in charge of the Asheville office.

That is where I first contacted him by phone in 2006, explaining that I, as a family member, was looking into the Frances Bullock murder case. Soon afterward we met in person at the Macon County Detention Center for an initial discussion, along with Major Andy Shields of the sheriff's department, who had an interest in the case.

When Moody retired he took a position as a special investigator with the sheriff's department.

Lt. Moody's interest and information would turn out to be very beneficial for getting a better insight into how the case might be solved, or at least bring the closure that was long overdue. He later told me he did not think he had all the official file information at that point after learning some of the information given in my Q&A session with the SBI counsel I attended in 2007.

Macon County Sheriff's Deputy Major Andy Shields also presented this case to a 1998 Applied Criminal Psychology case study class at the U.S. Marine Corps Criminal Investigative Division at Parris Island, South Carolina.

That class study shed more light on the psychology of major persons-of-interest in the Bullock homicide.

Major Shields has since explained to me the criteria for subjecting a person to a polygraph test. It involves evaluation of the person's mental and emotional status as part of the equation for determining the results, or if they even qualify for current testing procedures. Having a history of treatment for mental illness could be a major disqualifying factor.

In the years since the 1960s investigation, other SBI agents were assigned the unsolved Bullock murder, with the possibility that a new set of eyes might find something.

One was Agent James Maxey, who I met at another investigation when I was a radio reporter assigned to cover a missing child in the Highlands, North Carolina area. Agents Maxey and Harold Elliot, a Franklin native, were on that case. They both inherited the Bullock murder case along with agents Hess and Moody.

Being from the same hometown as Bullock, Agent Elliot was particularly interested in solving the case but was unable to with what he had to go on in the records.

Chapter 26

Dr. Henry C. Lee - SBI Legal Counsel

Dr. Henry C. Lee is a forensic expert known worldwide for his role in some high-profile cases such as the O.J. Simpson, Jon Benet Ramsey, and Scott Peterson cases. On a fluke chance he might help in the Frances Bullock case, I reached out to him. Surprisingly, he responded, and gave me some good advice that enabled me to get much more information.

```
Sun July 29, 2012 9:45 PM

Dear Mr. Evans,
Your letter to our institute has finally forward to me. I
am sorry to hear that there is nobody interested in re-
investigation of the death of Frances Bullock. Unfortuntly
many cases in US are under investigated during the early
stage of the case. In addition, there is a jurisdiction
issue about any investigation. Unless the local police
department fully cooperate and endorse a re-investigation,
otherwise very difficult to proceed.  There are only few
options available for you to re-open this case; you can ask
your Governor, AG or Congressman to intervene or to have a
lawyer to ask the police to release the file and evidence
to the family.
I wish you the best luck for seeking the justice for Mrs.
Bullock.
Dr. Henry Lee
```

Founder and professor of the Forensic Science Program
at the University of New Haven

North Carolina General Statute NCGS-132-1.4 protects unsolved SBI investigative records of cases in order to preserve the information from influence pending upcoming court procedures, and to keep confidential investigative techniques from jeopardizing ongoing or future cases.

As long as it is an unsolved murder case it remains open with the records concealed from the public and remain in the custody of the SBI.

Even after fifty years that statute still applies; however, I requested help from a former judge, John Snow of Murphy, who at the time was a North Carolina state senator.

I was seeking information about the investigation in order to see if there were areas the family could still contribute useful information, and at the same time bring closure for the family. I was interested in confirming or dispelling rumors of a coverup, and get to the truth in the matter, moving beyond the persistent rumors and gossip that had plagued this case from the beginning.

Snow contacted Robin Pendergraft, who was director of the SBI at the time, telling her about the plight of the family, and that he had been requested to introduce legislation to wave the statute in this case.

Director Pendergraft replied, "I sympathize with the family of Mrs. Bullock but feel that the release of the SBI investigative files would not be in the best interest of the public and the criminal justice system."

She proceeded to cite other reasons, among them how it would set precedence, and how current investigations of recent and future cases could become jeopardized.

She added; "However, I am willing to offer the Bullock family an opportunity to meet with our legal counsel, John Watters, if they are interested."

She would ask Watters to read the file entirely and answer questions submitted by the family. Hopefully, the family representative might have additional information that would help in solving the case.

I consulted with Frankie's niece, Faye Wells, and we decided to go forward with the director's offer and contacted John Watters, who had been made aware of the offer. He advised he would need ample time to retrieve the records, review them, and then work a meeting into his busy schedule representing other SBI requests.

On July 10, 2007 Faye Wells and I traveled to the SBI Regional Office in Hickory, North Carolina and met with Watters for what turned out to be an all-day session without a break for lunch.

While Watters had been reviewing the records from the SBI archives, we had the opportunity of several weeks to prepare long and short lists of questions.

The session with Watters was very revealing and productive.

We got most of our short list questions answered. We adjourned after a tiring day for us and Watters.

He would try to arrange for a follow-up interview, but that never took place.

In that session we learned the primary persons-of-interest and about their alibis; who took polygraph tests and the results; what evidence was tested at the SBI crime lab; and a description of the crime scene investigation. We learned the names of supportive witnesses to alibis that were given by subjects, the names of the investigators involved in the case, and about the autopsy of the victim.

Learning all the detailed investigative information gave us direction to follow up on our own.

Having a subject left alive to prosecute, should probable cause be discovered, is a big priority for the authorities in re-activating a case.

After fifty-five years it is most likely there is no one left alive to be prosecuted. Unless someone made a death bed confession to someone that can be substantiated, it is likely only scientific technology can solve the Bullock murder case now.

Chapter 27

Afterword

<u>Gordon Lee Forrester</u>, who had been engaged to marry Frances Bullock before she broke the engagement the week she was murdered, married another woman eight months after Frances Bullock's murder.

In April 1964 Evelyn Marie Dowdy, of Manteo, North Carolina, became Forrester's fourth wife. They lived in Elizabeth City, North Carolina, where he was still an IRS employee. They had a son, Mitchell Clifton Forrester, in 1966. Then, they were divorced in 1967, reportedly because of his abusive behavior.

Marie Dowdy Forrester returned to her hometown of Manteo, married again, and her son was adopted by his stepfather. She retired after 20 years as a dispatcher for the Dare County Sheriff's Department. She died in May, 2011. Her son had taken his stepfather's last name, and Cliff Davis still resides in Manteo. He has been previously arrested, charged, and convicted twice for assault.

When I spoke with Cliff Davis by phone, he said he was told that his real father died before he was born. He had lived with his grandmother and mother after her divorce from Gordon Forrester.

Cliff said he had been married and divorced with children living in town with their mother and stepfather. He added that he knew he had a half-brother living somewhere but had never met him.

So, when was the first marriage for Gordon Forrester? It was long ago, when he was very young and living in his hometown of Fredrick, Oklahoma.

In a recent check of old records I found there are official records of two very early marriage ceremonies in Oklahoma, both in 1939, between Gordon Lee Forrester,18, of Fredrick, Oklahoma, to Allene Barnes, 16, of Tipton, Oklahoma.

The first was in June when they lied about their age of him being 21 and her being 18. They married in nearby Greer County without parental consent. The second marriage was in November in her hometown of Tipton in Tillman County, Oklahoma, with her parents signing and agreeing to the union. Five months later, in the 1940 census, they were listed as living in the household of her father, Jess H. Barnes.

However, by November 1941, Allene, married R.T. Powell, in Altus, Oklahoma, using her maiden name of Allene Barnes.

I found no records of her divorce, annulment, or child birth records while married to Gordon Lee Forrester.

Just over a month after Allene's second marriage, Gordon Lee Forrester joined the U.S. Navy in January 1942, less than a month after the Pearl Harbor attack by Japan.

I lost track of Forrester for several years after his Elizabeth City divorce and before his death.

Gordon Forrester died at age 55, on March 8, 1977 in Louisiana.

The personal records as to marriage, birth, death, etc. are closely guarded in Louisiana, where I am told that much of the laws and statutes are based on the French Napoleonic law; whereas, much of the rest of the country has roots in English Common law.

Upon my inquiry, a local Ruston funeral home operator obtained the funeral details for Gordon Forrester. He died at a nearby hospital and was buried at Ruston's Forest Lawn Cemetery, where his second wife, Marjorie, is also buried. Their son, Geoffrey Forrester, lives in a nearby town in Louisiana.

<u>Charles K. "Charlie" Stanfield</u> requested and was given permission by the administrator of Frances Bullock's will and trust to take charge of selling Frankie's antiques and her 1962 Mercury Monterey car. Charlie, his wife, and stepdaughter moved in with his mother, Odessa Stanfield, for the time being, and continued their antiques shop business.

In October 1964 he and Hazel acquired some roadfront property from her parents, Chester and Martha Sizemore, south of Franklin in the Longview community. The deed stipulated a payment of $10, and other considerations were to allow the Sizemores to live in their own house on the property for life, take care of them in sickness, and pay their funeral expenses.Within four months of the deed transfer

Chester Sizemore died in February 1965, and Martha in November 1977.

Charlie Stanfield built a two-story, concrete block building next door to the Sizemore house, across from the present day Ruby Movie Theatres.

The new building served as an upstairs living quarters for the family, with a Texaco gas station and antiques shop downstairs. Some years later the widening of highway U.S. 441 made it necessary to sell the location to the state department of transportation, and the building was demolished.

They relocated further south to an old house where they continued to sell antiques. They had a daughter, born in 1967.

Their activities had been scrutinized by law enforcement for awhile, but they appeared to have lived out the remainder of their lives peacefully after the turmoil of 1963.

Longview Texaco   1956 black & white Bel Air Chevy
(family photo)

In February 1966, Wiley Rogers McConnell, 38, whose wife, Louise Sizemore McConnell, was Hazel Stanfield's sister, gave a statement to Sheriff Brice Rowland concerning events of what he remembered as being Friday night July 26, 1963. This statement came two-and-a-half years after the death of Frances Bullock.

In his statement he gave information that, if factual and accurate, could jeopardize Charlie and Hazel Stanfield's alibi they had given the investigators. The sheriff had to wonder why McConnell had waited so long to come forward with this information. There could have been a question as to the accuracy of McConnell's memory of the exact date and time. There could have been an issue over the Sizemore property that motivated this sudden disclosure. For whatever reason Sheriff Rowland did not deem it viable to reactivate the case.

Chester Sizemore had already died a year earlier in February 1965, and the statement was never fully verified. Both Wiley and Louise McConnell are also deceased. There is no record of McConnell's statement being further pursued.

Charlie Stanfield died unexpectedly of a heart attack in 1977 at age 50, and his wife Hazel died in 1996.

Doris Stanfield Townsend, Frankie's youngest sister, her husband and their sons were transferred back to

Colorado.

Tragedy struck the family once again when in January 1965, less than two years after Frankie's death, Doris took her own life. She died of carbon monoxide poisoning late at night in a car parked in their home garage. Her death was investigated for possible links to her sister Frankie's murder and there were none found.

From a note she allegedly left, her reason was more of a domestic marital nature, with no mention of her sister's murder, or the emotional effects it had on her.

Preparations for the burial back in North Carolina were ironically handled there in Littleton, Colorado by the Bullock Funeral Home — no relation to the Bullock's back in Franklin.

Doris's tragic death sent shock waves through the family. For her mother, Odessa, back in Franklin, the news was devastating. She already had tragically lost one daughter — and now another.

Nettie Mae Stanfield Lear and her husband, Robert, sold their dairy farm in New Jersey and moved to Franklin with their teenage daughter, Faye. They bought farm property and built a house in the Cartoogechaye community on what they called "The Lear Farm." Nettie Mae died in March 1988, and Robert ten years later in 1998. Their daughter, Faye Wells, now owns and lives in one of the three houses on the Lear Farm.

Nettie Mae's stepdaughter, Margaret, lives in

Pennsylvania and her other stepdaughter Betty, who remained in New Jersey, died in recent years.

Odessa F. Stanfield, had sadly outlived all her children. She had sold her house on the Highlands Road and built a new house at the Lear Farm near her daughter, Nettie Mae, and her family.

Odessa Stanfield died in January 1990 and is buried beside her husband, Grover Stanfield, and infant son, Billy, at the hillside Salem Church Cemetery in the Cullasaja community across the river from where she used to live. All their other children are buried at Woodlawn Cemetery in Franklin.

John H. Kusterer, the Macon County coroner in 1963, died unexpectedly at age 49 on November 30, 1963 of a heart attack (coronary thrombosis) around 8 a.m., according to his official death certificate signed by Dr. Edgar Angel of Franklin. It was just four months after Frances Bullock's death — adding more fodder to the rumor mill about the murder of Frances Bullock.

Kusterer's death left the coroner's position open. He had been elected as a Democrat and had served for six years. Dr. E.W. Fisher, MD of Franklin was appointed to succeed Kusterer. The doctor, upon examining the autopsy report and photos showing the victim's wounds, formed an inconclusive opinion that the weapon used in the murder could have been a scalpel.

A few days before Kusterer's death in November

1963 President John F. Kennedy was assassinated in Dallas, and the news coverage of that tragedy somewhat overshadowed the news of the Bullock murder case.

<u>Lt. Charles Moody</u>, after retiring from the North Carolina SBI, had join the Macon County Sheriff's Office as a special investigator. He had taken a special interest in the case when he was with his former agency.

In his new role, he re-examined the recently acquired Bullock murder evidence, especially the bloody dress, and found what could be evidence of blood from another donor dripped on the dress. The second donor could have been nicked while wielding the weapon during the attack on the victim and left a trace of blood on the dress.

If so, then modern technology might produce useful DNA that could be linked to the person. The dress was sent to the North Carolina SBI crime lab for the second time, and there several likely samples were cut from the dress and tested for DNA evidence; however, all samples proved to be that of the victim. In one way this was disappointing news, but at least an effort had been attempted that was appreciated by Frances Bullock's family, and it added new information to the case file.

In the meantime, on July 30, 2008, NC SBI Special Agent Duane Deaver reviewed the SBI Bullock case file concerning the principle persons-of-interest.

Deaver supposedly had experience in modern psychological profile techniques. He evaluated each person's past mental issues, alcohol abuse, interview responses, history of abusive behavior, facts in the case and arrived at a single likely suspect, but no probable cause to go forward.

However, Deaver's credability as a profiler is brought into question after he perjuried himself and was fired from the SBI in 2011, for withholding crucial evidence in his expert forensic testimony that contributed to the wrongful conviction of a man to life in prison. The man was released in 2014 after serving eight years in prison.

Deaver's dismissal brought about a "shake-up" of the SBI crime lab, and reassignment of the SBI director Pendergraft.

Paul Townsend, the ten-year-old nephew of Frances Bullock, who inherited her estate, received his total benefits. The house he inherited was sold to Laura M. Jones in 1968. Paul made some ill-fated investments in Colorado's ski tourist industry. Both his parents and brother Stan are deceased. He is retired and still lives in Colorado, where at last word his oldest brother, Allen, who suffered a debilitating stroke in the 1970s, is living with Paul and his family.

Laura Jones died in 1972, and her brother, Dr. J. Paul Jones, acquired the house. A brick extension was added to the south side of the house that became a third bedroom. The extension had incorporated Ebb Bullock's former den on that side of the house. Dr. Jones' daughter later received ownership of the house.

The house was unoccupied for almost ten years. It began to deteriorate. Knowing that a murder had taken place there, it became an attraction for Halloween pranksters who sometimes rallied at the so called "haunted house".

Former Franklin policeman David Houston said they received calls of vandalism at the house, which they investigated. Eventually the necessary renovations were made, restoring it to original condition, which is the way it is still maintained, nicely furnished and occupied today. The Halloween visits finally ceased once it became occupied again.

In 2007 Faye Wells and I were invited to visit inside the house for the first time since before Frankie's death. We found the house tastefully decorated and immaculate in a way that would have very much pleased our late relative Frances Bullock.

Lewis Clayton retired from the Detroit Board of Education and continued to lend financial and parental support to his mentally challenged son.

Charles Davidson had kept up with his cousin Frankie's murder case through the years. He died from cancer in 2003. Some of his notes were passed on to others; however, a journal he kept on Frances Bullock's murder has mysteriously disappeared. Upon my request, his wife Maxine came up with some legal pad notes he had taken of the letters to and from Frankie and Gordon Forrester that she turned over to me. Maxine Davidson died a few years ago.

Re-examining evidence

In 2014 I contacted crime scene forensic experts who, with permission from the sheriff's department, might consider examining the evidence using modern technology.

I had already reached out to Dr. Henry Lee, the well-known expert in forensic investigation, and he had responded with good advice.

My second contact with an expert was Karen L. Smith of CSI Academy of Florida after watching her in a PBS-TV documentary series about how the "Sherlock Holmes" books had led to modern day forensic investigative techniques. She was a narrator in the series, along with Lee, and she also demonstrated her expertise in analyzing blood splatter and castoff in that nationally televised series.

When I finally located her, and I told her of the unsolved fifty-year-old Frances Bullock murder and that the evidence still existed, she became very interested in helping.

She recently commented about that first encounter about the murder case.

"When Ronnie contacted me, his passion and

ambition to finally solve the murder of Frankie Bullock was palpable. How could I say no? The evidence was remarkably preserved and, working with Dr. Max Noureddine, we uncovered some new possibilities regarding the bloodstain patterns left behind on her pink dress. Perhaps this new information will help move the case forward after 55 years. It was a privilege to work with local law enforcement and my hat's off to them for allowing outsiders the opportunity to view and work on such a legendary case. I hope that one day the true perpetrator can be named and the case finally closed for good."

I also looked into other sources of expert help that were affordable. I was referred to Dr. Noureddine of ForensiGen, LLC in Greensboro, North Carolina. His expertise is well-known and respected by the North Carolina SBI Crime Lab. He was very willing to help in the matter of evidence re-examination.

Permission for viewing and examining the homicide evidence was granted by the Macon County Sheriff's Department with stipulations.

In August, 2014, after much coordination, Karen Smith from Florida, and Dr. Noureddine from Greensboro volunteered to meet with me in Franklin to review the case file I had assembled over recent years. I picked up the tab for their stay at a local hotel and took them out for dinner and lunch while they were here, where we informally discussed the case and had interesting casual conversation.

In a conference room at their hotel, after breakfast, we had a formal meeting to discuss the murder case file and autopsy. This would give them a better working knowledge of what to look for when presented the evidence. That meeting was scheduled a couple hours later at the Macon County Detention Center conference room, where the long-awaited supervised examination was set to take place.

The Macon County Sheriff Department had granted permission for the family to view and the evidence, for the very first time, and allow access to the experts who came volunteering their specialized services. Strict guidelines were explained by Chief Investigator Lt. Charles Moody, and with constant observation by Major Andy Shields and another deputy to assure chain-of-custody of the evidence. We could examine and photograph all the evidence in the Bullock case that had been stored for over fifty years.

On long tables at least two dozen large crime scene photos from that 1963 case were displayed for us to view, although we were not allowed to copy them. Those photographs were invaluable to the examiners analysis of the evidence compared to the photos in accessing their results.

Later family member Faye Wells, who had been out of town, viewed the crime scene photographs along with photos I had made of the evidence.

The fifty-year-old evidence was carefully presented and examined. Taking the necessary precautions to

Display of SBI photos
(R. Evans)

avoid contamination the forensic team and Lt. Moody wore sterile latex gloves throughout the exam. The evidence consisted of: the bloody pink Bobby Brooks house dress, undergarments, and the Italian sandals she was wearing when her body was discovered. In addition, the soiled sweater and stained washcloth found in the basement, and the kitchen knife with a six-inch blade that had been randomly taken from a kitchen utensil drawer were displayed.

Lt. Moody opens Bullock homicide evidence
(R. Evans photo)

Frankie - A Life Cut Short

Frankie and the dress and sandals she
was wearing when murdered

(photos this page R. Evans)

Two chemical tests were made on the fifty-year-old stained washcloth. The first one by Smith with luminol did not produce positive results; but a second, more advanced, forensic chemical test conducted by Dr. Noureddine did conclude it was blood on the washcloth. How and when the blood got there is still not known, and a DNA test was not performed. His test of the soiled sweater yielded no evidence of blood.

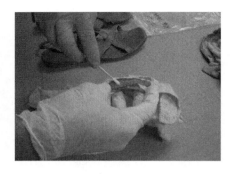

Testing the washcloth with luminol
(R. Evans photo)

After thoroughly examining and then bunching the dress fabric in the right shoulder area, the experts presented a reenactment of how the victim might have been attacked from behind. However, Lt. Moody indicated to me later this was not conclusive without taking into account the castoff blood and blood splatter in the kitchen of which, unfortunately, there are no photographs.

Karen L. Smith   Dr. Max Noureddine
(R .Evans photos)

Following the tests, Karen Smith, Lt. Charles Moody, and Maj. Andy Shields discussed other forensic possibilities.

Smith, who had been a police investigator before entering the academic ranks, suggested testing the hardwood flooring of the house for traces of a second donor's blood. Maj. Shields countered, with humor, that he did not think his sheriff would go along with the expense of replacing or repairing a hardwood floor unless there was a good chance of positive results.

Smith said she had done it before and got positive results, but there might be a way it could be done without doing any damage. It was something that had never been done before. She would have to prove it could be done first before pursuing it in this case.

Smith inquired if the same type of hardwood flooring was available.

"Yes," I answered, "it is still being manufactured in Franklin by Shaw Flooring Co., at the site of the original Zickgraf Hardwood Flooring Co."

Before an interview at The Franklin Press office, I accompanied her to the nearby Shaw showroom where she acquired some samples to take back to her lab in Florida.

"The finish for the flooring back in that time period was shellac," I informed her. That is how our floor was finished in the 1950s. I remembered the distinct odor of shellac.

She would have to pick up shellac back in Florida,

since even a quart-sized container would not be allowed on her flight from Atlanta.

Within a year, through documented scientific testing, she proved that she could obtain blood samples through the shellac finish without damaging the flooring. The results were published in the Journal of Forensic Identification sharing the new-found information with other forensic investigators. She gave me a copy of the book, which I shared with Lt. Moody.

Her Case Report in the Journal is titled "The Efficacy of Blue Star Forensic on Wood Floors Coated with Lacquer and Shellac: Cold Case in Progress."

In the report, Smith, working with Bare Bones Consulting, LLC and CSI Academy of Florida, referred to the 1963 cold case investigation and evidence examination in Franklin. She gives the basic description of the attack and the investigation. She praises the condition of the evidence that she was shown in a re-examination 51 years after the murder.

Her proven tests were based on that case and could have far-reaching results for similar future cases.

Lt. Moody and I discussed if that technique could be used in the Bullock case on the hardwood floors to detect traces of blood in the Bullock house. Probably, but it would be nearly impossible to establish when those stains might have occurred unless there was an official record or witness to the exact spot where it was found. Since there is none, it was not pursued.

Dr. Noureddine had some information about testing for "touch DNA" of the victim's dress.

In his opinion, even after fifty years the assailant's DNA could still be there. It would depend if the evidence had been properly stored in a manner that would not contaminate the sampled area. Some contamination could be expected after being handled by so many authorities and technicians long before the science of touch DNA was ever possible or considered. He added, that even stored in paper bags, which is standard, during the fifty years dust particles from one area could float to another and contaminate the test areas.

New technology for touch DNA is expensive; therefore, to get the ball rolling Noureddine volunteered to pay for one lab fee ($500) if funding could be obtained for perhaps two dozen or more others that would be required. His gracious offer was appreciated, but I was informed there was no funding on that scale available in the Macon County Sheriff Department's or district attorney's budgets at this time. There are no family resources available as well to conduct the tests.

For positive proof, touch DNA would also have to produce someone who would not have normally come in direct contact with the victim. In Frances Bullock's case, the prime persons-of-interest, who were often in her presence, could have touched her when she was wearing that dress other than during the murder timeline.

The chance of getting positive results would be a long shot. This idea was abandoned —for now.

It appears the investigation of the 1963 murder of Frances Elizabeth "Frankie" Bullock has come to a halt, in order to let technology catch up before going forward again.

In July 2018 I received a message from forensic investigator Smith, informing me that she now lives in Los Angeles. She is a forensic expert for numerous national television and radio programs, and still maintains a high interest in the unsolved murder of Frances S. Bullock and hopes to use it in upcoming national presentations she wants to discuss with me as plans are developed.

Postscript

Much of the custom-made E.S. Purdom furniture from Frances Bullock's house, including the dining room table, is now in the home of Frankie's niece, Faye Lear Wells.

A framed print of A.H. Sonn's painting "Red Cloud" was on the living room wall facing the dining room the night Frankie was killed. It was given as a memento to my family.

If only Red Cloud could speak, what a story he could tell.

Framed print from Frankie's
living room wall

Ronald C. Evans

I have written what I believe to be the factual truth. The narrative is derived from a twelve-year culmination of information gathered from various sources enabling me to purvey this historic nonfiction life and death story.

Through this experience I have been enlightened about the homicide and what led up to it, as well as the injustices of domestic violence and abuse.

Thus far justice for Frances Bullock has been alluded, and someone absolutely got away with murder.

On Friday afternoon July 26, 2013 at Woodlawn Cemetery, after fifty years, the final inscription on the grave site monument for "Frances" Bullock was completed.

Frankie's niece Faye Wells placed a hand-picked bouquet of wild flowers from the Lear Farm at the grave to commemorate the occasion.

"Frankie - A Life Cut Short"

Ronald C. Evans

About the Author

Ronald C. "Ronnie" Evans is a retired television engineer, a performing musician, and now a first-time author. His previous writing experience was limited to writing commercial copy and news reports when working in radio, and assisting writing grants for equipment in television.

He is a native of Franklin, where he still resides with his artist wife, Jean. He is a musician with several recordings of his guitar music.

His Macon County family roots go back over five generations. He is an Army veteran, having served during the Vietnam War era.

After retirement from UNC-TV Engineering he became interested in family genealogy; which has been an aid in his writing experience, having shared the same ancestral background with many of the persons mentioned in the book, including the victim, Frances S. Bullock.

Ronald C. Evans

Contact information about the book:

Ronald C. Evans
PO Box 134
Franklin, NC 28744

Ronald C. Evans